WHAT'S NEW, CUPCAKE?

WHAT'S NEW,

CUPCAKE?

Karen Tack and Alan Richardson

TEXT AND PHOTOGRAPHS BY ALAN RICHARDSON
RECIPES AND FOOD STYLING BY KAREN TACK

HOUGHTON MIFFLIN HARCOURT
Boston New York 2010

To my mom and dad, who believe that
every meal should end with dessert—even breakfast.
　　　—K.T.

In memory of my mom, who never cooked
a meal she didn't like—and she was right.
　　　—A.R.

Visit our website: www.hmhbooks.com

For information about permission to reproduce selections from this book, write to Permissions, Houghton Mifflin Harcourt Publishing Company, 215 Park Avenue South, New York, New York 10003.

Book design by Michaela Sullivan • Typeface: Helvetica Neue

Copyright © 2010 by Karen Tack and Alan Richardson

Printed in the United States of America • DOW 10 9 8 7 6

Library of Congress
　Cataloging-in-Publication Data
　Tack, Karen.
　　What's new, cupcake? : ingeniously simple
　designs for every occasion / Karen Tack and
　Alan Richardson ; text and photographs by
　Alan Richardson ; recipes and food styling
　by Karen Tack.
　　p. cm.
　ISBN 978-0-547-24181-4
　1. Cupcakes. 2. Cake decorating.
　I. Richardson, Alan, date. II. Title.
　TX771.T322 2010
　641.8'653—dc22
　2009050646

Acknowledgments

So many people helped us make *Hello, Cupcake!* a success, and so many more have helped us create *What's New, Cupcake?* We are lucky to have families that are both patient and talented. The Tack family has lived with cupcakes up to their eyeballs for countless months. Chris Tack supports us, cheers us on, and advises us on every project, every step of the way. Erik and Liam Tack mostly assist by ignoring our insanity but also chime in with the necessary "Awesome!" when we get it right. We rely on Larry Frascella as our trusted barometer, always letting us know when our cupcakes are too weird or when our words don't make sense. Thanks to all of you for everything—we love you.

Our support team at our publishing house has been amazing. We have an insightful editor, Rux Martin, who keeps us on our toes at all times. We are also grateful to Rux and her partner, Barry Estabrook, for letting Elvis and Presley, their dachshunds, pose for our cupcakes. Our art director, Michaela Sullivan, always makes our work look gorgeous. Our amazing marketing and publicity team, Bridget Marmion, Lori Glazer, Katrina Kruse, Alia Habib, and Joanna Pinsker, has brought us to heights we never expected. Ryan Kelly, Ron Hussey, Teresa Elsey, Jacinta Monniere, Valerie Cimino, Susan Dickinson, Gail Cohen, Lisa Diercks, and so many others, we couldn't do it without you.

Many thanks to our friend Deb Donahue for rescuing us with props whenever we started to run low.

We don't know if Martha Kaplan is the wisest agent on earth or the most diligent nanny, but either way she seems to always be watching out for us. We can't thank you enough, Martha.

We have had terrific support from so many surprising sources. Kathie Lee Gifford and Hoda Kotb at Today have been on the cupcake train from the beginning. Producer Brian Balthazar was an early believer and did so much to help us. Paula Deen and Brandon Branch have been amazingly generous with their support. Sandy Ploy and Rachel Bussel blog their joy in cupcaking every day, and we are grateful they have taken us along for the ride. Thanks to Nathalie Reid for making it her mission to get everyone in America to take a cupcaking class with us. Dorie Greenspan, Carol Prager, Maria McBride, Mark Bittman, Susan Westmoreland, Linda Fears, Karmen Lizzul, Jane Chestnut, Jackie Plant, Sally Lee, Babs Chernetz, Karen Cicero, Marisol Vera, Catherine Cassidy, Ardith Cope, Sarah Thompson, Stephanie Saible, Chris Koury, Karen Tanaka, and so many more friends in our publishing family have offered their support and continue to help us every day. We appreciate everything you've done.

And to all the wonderful readers, eaters, and new friends who have welcomed our cupcakes into their homes, hearts, and yes, stomachs, all we can say is thank you. Every time we hear your cupcake stories, it gives us a thrill. So cheers to you all, and keep on cupcaking.

CONTENTS

They Thought We Were Nuts...

When we painted "Starry Night" on a canvas of cupcakes using nothing more than tinted frosting and a ziplock bag, they said we were as looney as van Gogh himself. When we used candy and snacks from the grocery store to turn our cupcakes into howling werewolves, bowling pins, penguins, and sharks, they thought we had lost our minds. But when we served spaghetti and meatballs made from chocolate candies and strawberry jam—with a side order of corn on the cob fashioned from jelly beans and taffy—everyone wanted to join in the fun.

Our new cupcake creations are spectacular—and even easier than the ones in our first book, *Hello, Cupcake!* You'll find cupcakes for every occasion, from a take-out pizza that delivers plenty of April Fool's Day laughs to a Formula One race car that will fast-lane the birthday party fun. Surprise a new mom with a shower of cupcake babies, give your sweetheart a dozen long-stemmed cupcake roses, bring the teacher a bright red cupcake apple for the first day of school, scare the trick-or-treaters with creepy caramel cockroach cupcakes, or bake up a festive gingerbread village for the holidays—anything others do with gingerbread, you can do better with gingerbread cupcakes.

If your cooking inclinations lean more toward takeout than rolling out dough, don't worry. We've given you lots of EZ Cupcakes, including beautiful mums for Mother's Day and pies for a bake sale that will make you look like the most talented pastry chef around. We also show you how to doctor store-bought cake mixes with brand-new flavors like chocolate mint and orange spice and provide you with our patented "almost homemade" buttercream frosting in seven new flavors, from espresso to raspberry.

So what's new, Cupcake? Turn the page, pick a project, and prepare yourself for the most candyful and creative cupcakes ever.

So many ways to decorate . . .

With so many ways to use candy to decorate a cupcake, there's never a reason to be without an ingredient. Need a leaf? Try green Swedish Fish, spearmint leaves, or a candy fruit slice. Haven't got them? You can make almost anything from taffy. Check the pantry and fire up your imagination.

pick a flower   pick a leaf   pick a petal   pick a grass

Try a candy swap

Flower Power (page 63)

Anatomy of an  CUPCAKE

A few ingredients
+ simple techniques
= cupcakes anyone can make.

(You'll find EZ Cupcakes in every chapter.)

Cupcaking Materials, Tools, and Techniques

Koi Pond (page 99)

Bake-Sale Pies (page 49)

Ants on a Picnic (page 110)

Designer Candies

Small, colorful candies are perfect for creating a border, outlining a shape, or making a whimsical design.

Alternate colors to create a border.

Arrange in abstract patterns.

Create whimsical mosaics.

Mimic animals and objects.

Roller Candies

Taffy, chews, and sugared jellies are soft enough to be combined, shaped, rolled, and cut, giving them limitless design possibilities.

- Place taffy in the microwave for no more than 3 seconds to soften.

- Combine and roll out taffy to make thin sheets of colorful candy.

- Roll out jellies in sugar, using more sugar on top as needed to prevent sticking.

- Combine spice drops or jellies to make larger shapes.

- Cut with scissors, pinking shears, cookie cutters, or a paring knife.

Flex Candies

Flexible candies can be twisted, bent, or cut to make fanciful designs.

Tie knots, bend, and shape.

Cut fruit rolls to create flat shapes with color.

Snip or cut marshmallows, gum, and Circus Peanuts.

Essential Tools for Cupcaking

wax paper

copy paper

freezer-weight
ziplock bags
(1 quart and 1 pint)

food coloring

craft paper

toothpicks

regular scissors

offset tweezers

metal craft strips

craft scissors

offset spatula

craft tweezers

small rolling pin

wooden skewers

rubber spatula

transparent tape

small paintbrushes

small serrated knife

colored cupcake liners

ruler

pastry wheel

Filling Cupcake Liners

To avoid dribbling batter and to make it easy to get the same amount in every paper liner, use a freezer-weight ziplock bag.

• Use two 1-quart freezer-weight ziplock bags to hold 1 standard recipe mix.

• Place ziplock bags in separate plastic containers large enough to support them and fold the edges back over the containers.

• Divide the batter evenly between the bags, press out the excess air, and seal.

• Grasp the bag below the zipper, push the batter down to one corner, and snip ½ inch from the corner.

• Put the cut opening in the center of a liner, squeeze gently, fill two-thirds full, stop squeezing, lift, and repeat with the remaining liners.

• Use a rubber spatula to squeegee the last bit of batter down to the corner for piping.

Frosting Cupcakes

For a smooth experience, keep the frosting at room temperature and stir before using. And remember, less is never more.

Start by mounding a large dollop in the center and push to the edges.

Push the frosting in one direction while turning the cupcake in the opposite direction.

Swipe the top to remove any excess frosting and smooth the top.

For a peak, use the tip of an offset spatula to swirl and lift the frosting.

Filling a Ziplock Bag

Be sure to use freezer-weight bags because they can take the pressure when you squeeze.

• Invert the bag over your open hand and press to make a cup inside your fingers.

• Fill the cup inside your fingers with frosting and then lift the edges of the bag up and around the frosting.

• Press out the excess air and seal the bag.

• Use scissors to snip a corner according to the recipe.

Piping Frosting

THE SQUEEZE-RELEASE-PULL TECHNIQUE FOR GRASS, FUR, AND PETALS

Touch the tip of the bag to the surface, squeeze, and anchor the frosting. Release the pressure before lifting. Pull away to make a peak.

THE ANCHOR-FLY-ANCHOR TECHNIQUE FOR "FLYING" STRAIGHT LINES

Touch the tip of the bag to the surface, squeeze, and anchor the frosting. Pull up and away while continuing to squeeze, creating a "flying" straight line. Let the line drop into place, stop squeezing, and anchor it at the end.

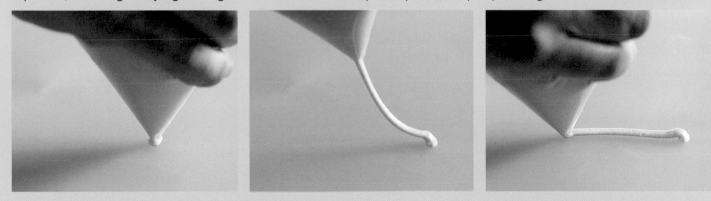

THE SQUEEZE-DRAG TECHNIQUE FOR BEADING

Touch the tip of the bag to the surface, squeeze a dot, and drag it. Lift the tip and return directly next to the first dot. Squeeze another dot and drag it, repeating in a straight line to make beading.

Building Cupcake Shapes

Snacks and candies hidden under the frosting of our cupcakes give them unexpected shapes.

Use a marshmallow, doughnut hole, and cupcake for a duck.

Frost the cupcake and press the shapes into the frosting.

Fill in the gaps at the edges and place in the freezer to chill.

Coating Cupcakes

After chilling, cupcakes can be finished any way you choose.

Cover with frosting for a textured look.

Coat in coconut for a fuzzy look.

Dip in melted frosting for a shiny look.

Dipping Cupcakes

Dipping cupcakes in melted canned frosting is one of those techniques that look amazingly sophisticated but are really easy to do. Canned frostings hold up well to heat and firm up nicely into a smooth sheen when they cool. Avoid the low-sugar or whipped varieties, as they tend to fall apart when heated.

Microwave the frosting according to the recipe. The best test for texture is to dip a spoon into the frosting and let it run back into the cup. It should have the texture of lightly whipped cream.

Chill the cupcake assemblies first to keep them from separating in the warm frosting. Hold a chilled cupcake by its paper bottom and dip the top into the melted frosting as directed in the recipe.

Use a spoon to ladle additional frosting over hard-to-reach areas. Lift the cupcake and allow the excess frosting to drip off before inverting and placing it aside to set.

Tinting Sugars, Nonpareils, Sprinkles, and Coconut

• Place the sugar, nonpareils, sprinkles, coconut, or other material in a ziplock bag.

• Add a few drops of food coloring to the bag. You can create new colors by mixing basic colors, like yellow and red to make orange.

• Seal the bag and shake until the sugar or other ingredient is evenly tinted.

Spread the tinted ingredient on wax paper to dry.

Store dried tinted sugar or other items in a sealed container until ready to use.

Edging and Coating Cupcakes

TO EDGE
A CUPCAKE

Place the coating material in a shallow bowl large enough to accommodate the cupcake. Hold the bowl at an angle and gently roll the edge in the coating material.

TO COAT
A CUPCAKE

Lightly press the frosting into the coating material to coat and shape the entire surface.

Drawing with Chocolate

Candy melting wafers melt and harden just like chocolate and are easier to handle. They come in a variety of colors and make custom shapes and designs a cinch.

• Place the chocolate melting wafers in a ziplock bag; do not seal. Microwave for 10 seconds, check to be sure the bag is not too hot to handle, massage the bag to smooth the chocolate, and microwave for another 10 seconds, massaging to remove all lumps. Repeat as necessary.

• Press out the excess air, seal the bag, and push the melted candy down to one corner.

• Snip off a small corner of the ziplock bag as directed in the recipe.

• Place wax paper over the template, pipe the outline of the template, and then fill in the center of the shape.

• Tap the work surface gently to settle and smooth the chocolate drawing.

Add decorations such as nonpareils before the chocolate hardens.

Use a back-and-forth motion to create zigzag patterns for pine needles.

Supports for Candies and Cookies

Sandwich a pretzel between vanilla wafers using melted white chocolate for the glue.

Glue pretzels to the back of a cookie using melted chocolate.

Push pretzels directly into soft candies like spice drops and soft taffy.

Glue pretzels together using melted white chocolate to make a split-rail fence.

Press pretzels into cookie dough before baking, and bake in place.

Cupcaking with Custom Cookie Shapes

• Start with store-bought sugar cookie or chocolate cookie dough from the refrigerator case. (See Quick Sugar Cookie recipes, page 225.)

• Incorporate flour (for sugar cookies) or unsweetened cocoa powder (for chocolate cookies) and roll out on wax paper.

• Cut out the cookies, transfer to a cookie sheet, and bake according to the package directions.

For more intricate shapes, or when you need a lot of cookies, bend 1/2-inch metal strips (available at craft stores) into shapes to match the templates and tape the ends to create custom cookie cutters.

Lids, straws, and other common kitchen items can also be useful for cutting cookies.

To make simple shapes, or if you need only a few cookies, use a small knife to follow the template and cut out the cookies.

Cupcaking with Melted Hard Candy

• Place the candies in a freezer-weight ziplock bag.

• Use the back of a pan, a rolling pin, or a hammer to break the candy into small, but not powder-fine, pieces.

• Place the crushed candy in an even layer on a foil-lined cookie sheet and bake in a 350°F oven until just melted and smooth, 3 to 4 minutes.

• While the candy is still soft, press oiled metal cutters into it, leave them in place, and allow to cool completely.

• Gently break the shapes from the cooled candy sheet.

You can also fill prebaked cookie shapes with crushed candy and bake for a few minutes more to melt the candy.

April Fool's Play

French fries from pound cake, a banana with crunch, foot-longs with spice drops and taffy for lunch. Lo mein with fruit chews may sound gourmet, but think twice before eating—it's April Fool's Day. These cupcakes are the perfect foil for birthdays, holidays, sleepovers, or any time you need a laugh.

vanilla frosting

pound cake

red food coloring

SIDE OF FRIES

ez
CUPCAKE

Want fries with that? Our clever crinkle-cuts are made from pound cake lightly toasted to look as though they're right out of the fryer. If you prefer straight-cut fries, just slice them into long, thin strips and toast them up. Squirt on the frosting ketchup, and these fries are ready for the drive-up window.

4 **mini vanilla cupcakes baked in white paper liners**

10 **vanilla cupcakes baked in white paper liners**

1 **frozen pound cake (10.75 ounces; Sara Lee), thawed**

1 **can (16 ounces) vanilla frosting**

Red food coloring (use paste coloring for a darker red; Wilton)

Plastic squeeze bottle (optional)

Extra red frosting for ketchup bottle (optional)

1. Trim the ends of the pound cake. Cut the pound cake into ½-inch-thick slices. Using a crinkle vegetable cutter (see Sources), cut the pound cake crosswise into ½-inch-wide strips. Transfer the strips to two cookie sheets and spread in a single layer.

2. Preheat the broiler to high. Toast the pound cake strips under the broiler until golden, 20 to 30 seconds. Turn the pieces and continue toasting until all sides are golden. Repeat with the other cookie sheet. Transfer to a wire rack to cool.

3. Tint ¼ cup of the vanilla frosting bright red with the red food coloring. For the ketchup, spread the red frosting on top of the mini cupcakes and smooth. Spread the tops of the standard cupcakes with the

remaining vanilla frosting to cover. Arrange the cooled fries on top of the vanilla-frosted standard cupcakes, 4 to 6 fries per cupcake. Arrange the cupcakes in a cardboard container or on a platter with the red-frosted mini cupcakes. Serve with more red frosting in a squeeze bottle, if desired.

HOLD THE ANCHOVIES

One large pizza to go. Pile on the pepperoni (fruit leather), bring on the sausage (chocolate cookies), don't forget the sauce (red frosting)—and make it with extra cheese (grated white chocolate). And be sure to brown that crust with cocoa powder.

19 vanilla cupcakes baked in white paper liners

8 ounces white chocolate chips

1 can (16 ounces) plus 1/2 cup vanilla frosting

1 teaspoon unsweetened cocoa powder

Yellow and red food coloring

2 rolls strawberry fruit leather (Fruit by the Foot)

10 thin chocolate cookies (Famous Chocolate Wafers)

1/3 cup chocolate-covered raisins (Raisinets)

1 package (0.9 ounce) small round chocolate cookies (Gripz)

1 medium pizza box (optional)

1. Melt the white chocolate chips in a microwavable bowl in the microwave for about 1 minute, stopping to stir frequently, until smooth. Spoon the melted chocolate into a small plastic or foil container (about 2 by 4 inches and 2 inches deep). Smooth the top and refrigerate until set, about 20 minutes. When set, remove from the container and let stand at room temperature.

2. Tint 1 1/4 cups of the vanilla frosting light brown with 1/2 teaspoon of the cocoa powder and a few drops of yellow food coloring. Spoon the frosting into a zip-lock bag, press out the excess air, and seal. Tint the remaining 3/4 cup frosting red with the food coloring. Place the red frosting in a microwavable bowl; cover with plastic wrap.

3. For the pepperoni, cut the fruit leather into as many 1-inch circles as possible using the back of a pastry tip, a small cookie cutter, or scissors. For the cheese,

place a box grater on top of a sheet of wax paper and grate about half of the block of white chocolate on the largest openings.

4. Arrange the cupcakes on a serving platter or in a pizza box, if desired (we ask our local pizza parlor for a pizza box; we get it for free). Place 1 cupcake in the center. Surround the cupcake with 6 more cupcakes and surround those with the 12 remaining cupcakes to make a pizza-size circle. Press the cupcakes as close together as possible.

5. Using a serrated knife, cut 6 of the chocolate wafer cookies in half. Using scissors, snip a small corner from the bag with the light brown frosting. Pipe a small amount of frosting on each corner of the cookie semicircle and use frosting to adhere the cookie, rounded side out, between 2 cupcakes on the outer edge. Repeat to fill in all the gaps, making a continuous outer edge. Cut the remaining 4 wafer cookies into pieces that will cover any of the remaining openings in the center of the cupcake assembly to make a solid surface. Attach the cookie pieces with a small amount of frosting.

6. Snip a larger ($1/2$-inch) corner from the bag with the light brown frosting. For the crust, pipe a steady line of frosting along the outer edge. Use a small spatula to blend the inside edge of the frosting crust onto the cupcakes.

7. Microwave the red frosting to soften slightly, 3 to 5 seconds. For the sauce, spoon the red frosting in the center of the cupcake circle and spread to the edge of the crust circle, creating a few swirls for texture.

8. Sprinkle the top of the red frosting with the grated white chocolate. Arrange the fruit leather pepperoni all over. For the sausage, add the chocolate-covered raisins and the small chocolate cookies in small clusters. Grate more white chocolate, if desired. Place the remaining $1/2$ teaspoon cocoa powder in a fine sieve and lightly dust a few areas on the crust for that pizza-oven color.

FAUX FOOT-LONG

Twelve inches of deli-fresh ham, cheese, lettuce, tomato, onion, and pickles layered on a seeded hero says April Fool's as only candy can. Our meat and cheese are made from fruit chews, the onions are cut from spice drops, the tomato is a fruit slice, and the lettuce leaves are cereal flakes tossed in green frosting. The hero itself? Cake doughnut sticks with sesame seeds.

4 vanilla cupcakes baked in white paper liners

1 cup corn or rice cereal flakes

1 cup canned vanilla frosting

Green food coloring

8 yellow fruit chews (Laffy Taffy, Starburst, Tootsie Fruit Rolls)

12 pink fruit chews (Laffy Taffy, Starburst, Jolly Rancher)

2 red candy fruit slices

2 tablespoons granulated sugar

6 white spice drops

2 plain cake doughnut sticks (6–8 inches long; Dunkin' Donuts)

1 teaspoon light corn syrup

2 teaspoons sesame seeds

3 green gumdrops (Dots)

Crispy apple chips (Seneca; optional)

1. Place the cereal in a medium bowl. Spoon 1 tablespoon vanilla frosting into a small ziplock bag, press out the excess air, and seal. Tint ¼ cup of the vanilla frosting green with the green food coloring. Heat the green frosting in a microwavable bowl in the microwave, stopping to stir frequently, until it has the texture of lightly whipped cream, about 15 seconds. Pour the frosting over the

cereal and toss well to coat. Spread the coated cereal on a cookie sheet in an even layer and refrigerate until set, about 15 minutes.

2. For the cheese, microwave the yellow fruit chews for 2 to 3 seconds to soften. Press 2 fruit chews together and roll out on a clean work surface into a rectangle about $1/8$ inch thick. Cut into a $1^1/_2$-by-2 inch rectangle. Continue with the remaining yellow fruit chews, rerolling scraps, to make a total of 6 rectangles. For the holes in the cheese, cut out small circles in the rectangles using an apple corer, a pastry tip, or a small round cookie cutter. For the ham, microwave the pink fruit chews for 2 to 3 seconds to soften. Press 2 fruit chews together and roll out on a clean work surface into a circle about $1/8$ inch thick. Cut each circle in half to make 12 semicircles.

3. For the tomatoes, cut each red fruit slice in half crosswise to make 2 thin slices. Sprinkle the work surface with some of the granulated sugar. For the onions, roll out the white spice drops $1/8$ inch thick, adding more sugar as necessary to prevent sticking. Cut out $1/8$-inch-wide onion rings using various sizes of small round cookie cutters, lids, pastry tips, or scissors, making as many rings as you can cut. For the hero-roll tops, cut $1/2$ inch from the bottom of the doughnut sticks; discard the bottom portion. Place the trimmed doughnut sticks, cut side down, on the work surface and cut each crosswise into two $2^1/_2$- to 3-inch pieces. Remove $1/4$ inch from the rounded ends of 2 of the pieces. Brush the tops with the corn syrup and sprinkle with the sesame seeds. For the pickle slices, flatten the green gumdrops with a rolling pin into rounds. Trim the edges with a small scalloped cookie cutter or decorative scissors. For the pickle seeds, snip a very small corner from the bag with the vanilla frosting and pipe small white dots in the center of each pickle slice.

4. Spread the tops of the cupcakes with the remaining vanilla frosting. Arrange the green cereal along the outer edge of the cupcakes as the lettuce. Add a red fruit slice as the tomato and a few onion rings made of spice drops to each cupcake. Add a few slices of cheese. Gather the straight sides of the pink fruit chews to create wavy ham slices and place on top of the cheese slices. Arrange the cupcakes in a row on a serving platter. Top with the doughnut sticks, untrimmed rounded pieces at the ends, to make the bread. Serve with the pickle slices and apple chips, if desired.

ALL CRACKED UP

People crack up every time they see these cupcakes. First we paint the inside of plastic pull-apart Easter eggs with white chocolate to make the eggshells. Then we break a few and put them on top of mini cupcakes. To make sure everyone gets the yolk, we add a dollop of lemon curd. What a great idea for breakfast on April Fool's Day.

12 mini vanilla cupcakes baked in white paper liners

1 cup white candy melting wafers (Wilton)

2 teaspoons vegetable oil

$^1/_2$ cup prepared lemon curd

Yellow and red food coloring

1 cup canned vanilla frosting

7 plastic Easter eggs (3$^1/_2$ inches long; see Sources)

1 clean egg carton (optional)

1. Place the white candy wafers in a microwavable bowl. Microwave for 10 seconds and stir. Repeat this process until the candies are melted and smooth, about 1 minute total.

2. Line a cookie sheet with wax paper and place in the refrigerator. Lightly oil a paper towel with the vegetable oil. Rub the inside of each plastic egg half with the oiled paper towel. Using your finger or a small brush, generously coat the inside of an oiled plastic egg half with the melted candy. Transfer the egg, open side down, to the cookie sheet in the refrigerator. Repeat with the remaining melted candy and plastic eggs. After a few minutes, check and touch up any eggs where the candy is too thin or there is a hole. Return to the refrigerator until set, about 5 minutes.

3. Carefully remove the hardened candy from the plastic eggs without breaking it (you will need 6 to 9 whole egg halves, plus any broken pieces for finishing).

4. Tint the lemon curd egg yolk yellow with 1 drop of red and 5 drops of yellow food coloring. Spoon the tinted lemon curd into a small ziplock bag, press out the excess air, and seal.

5. Spread the tops of the cupcakes with the vanilla frosting and smooth. Snip a small (^{1}/8-inch) corner from the bag with the lemon curd. For the egg yolks, pipe a small mound of lemon curd on top of each of the frosted cupcakes. For the whole eggs, place the candy eggshells, open side down, on top of the lemon curd to cover. For the broken eggs, arrange broken pieces of shells around the yolk. Place the cupcakes in the clean egg carton if using.

CHINESE TAKEOUT

House Special: Pork Lo Mein and Vegetarian Fried Rice. The kids will love this broccoli: green fruit chews with green frosting and nonpareils on a pile of lo mein noodles made of frosting squeezed from a ziplock bag. Serve fried rice on the side: puffed rice cereal tossed with fruit chews and jelly beans. And don't forget the caramel fortune cookies.

LO MEIN

6 vanilla cupcakes baked in white paper liners

6–8 green fruit chews (Jolly Rancher, Laffy Taffy)

3 pink fruit chews (Jolly Rancher, Starburst, Laffy Taffy)

1¹/₂ cups canned vanilla frosting

Green and yellow food coloring

1 teaspoon unsweetened cocoa powder (Hershey's)

¹/₂ cup dark green sprinkles (see Sources)

1 strand green licorice twist (Twizzlers Rainbow Twists), thinly sliced diagonally

Large Chinese food take-out containers (optional; see Sources)

1. Line a cookie sheet with wax paper. For the broccoli stems, make a lengthwise slit halfway down the center of each green fruit chew and open slightly. Place the stems on the prepared cookie sheet. Microwave the pink fruit chews for 2 to 3 seconds to soften. Press the pink fruit chews together and roll out into a 2-by-3-inch rectangle about ¹/₈ inch thick. For the pork slivers, cut the flattened fruit chew rectangle crosswise into ¹/₈-inch-wide strips.

2. Tint ¹/₂ cup of the vanilla frosting bright green with the green food coloring, spoon the frosting into a ziplock bag, press out the excess air, and seal. Tint 2 teaspoons of the remaining vanilla frosting with ¹/₂ teaspoon of the cocoa powder and 1 teaspoon water and mix to make a smooth brown paste. Tint the remaining vanilla frosting light brown with 1 drop of yellow food coloring and the

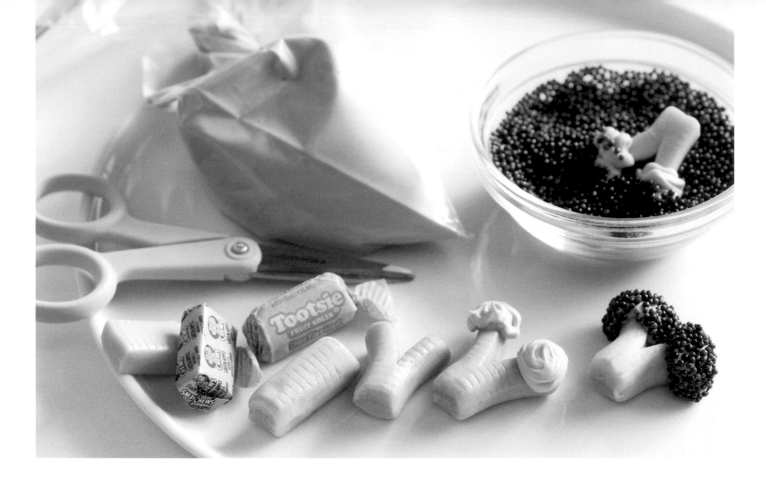

remaining ¹/₂ teaspoon cocoa powder. Spread the darker brown paste down the side of a ziplock bag and then fill in with the light brown frosting. Press out the excess air and seal.

3. Place the green sprinkles in a small bowl. Snip a small (¹/₈-inch) corner from the bag with the green frosting. For the broccoli florets, pipe mounds of frosting on the tips of the split ends of the green fruit chews on the cookie sheet. Holding the broccoli by the stem, press the frosted end lightly into the sprinkles to cover completely; return to the cookie sheet (see the photo above).

4. Snip a small (¹/₈-inch) corner from the bag with the brown frosting. To make the lo mein noodles, pipe the frosting in an irregular pattern all over the cupcakes, piling it high and letting it hang over the edges (the darker brown frosting will look like soy sauce). Arrange the pink fruit chew pork slivers randomly on top of the cupcakes. Add one or two pieces of broccoli on top. For scallions, scatter a few green licorice slices on top of the cupcakes.

5. To get the full effect, carefully place the cupcakes in the Chinese take-out containers, if using.

6 vanilla cupcakes baked in white paper liners

2 tablespoons small light green jelly beans (Jelly Belly)

4 orange fruit chews (Tootsie Fruit Rolls)

3 yellow fruit chews (Tootsie Fruit Rolls, Starburst)

1¼ cups puffed rice cereal (Rice Krispies)

1¼ cups canned vanilla frosting

¼ teaspoon unsweetened cocoa powder

2 strands green licorice twists (Twizzlers Rainbow Twists), thinly sliced diagonally

2 tablespoons chocolate sauce (optional)

1. For the peas, cut the green jelly beans in half crosswise with a small knife or clean scissors. For the carrots, cut the orange fruit chews into ¼-inch cubes. For the scrambled egg, cut the yellow fruit chews into small strips and pinch to soften the sharp edges. For the rice, place the rice cereal in a medium bowl.

2. Tint the vanilla frosting pale beige with the cocoa powder. Spread the tops of the cupcakes with a thin layer of frosting; use about ½ cup of the frosting. Heat the remaining ¾ cup frosting in a small microwavable bowl in the microwave until it has the texture of lightly whipped cream, about 15 seconds. Pour the heated frosting over the cereal, tossing to coat evenly. Reserve a few of the cut jelly beans and fruit chews for finishing and toss the rest with the cereal mixture. Spoon about ¼ cup of the cereal mixture on top of each frosted cupcake, pressing down to secure. Arrange the reserved candy pieces on top of the cupcakes. For the scallions, scatter a few licorice pieces on top.

3. Carefully place the cupcakes in large Chinese take-out containers, if using.

4. For the soy sauce, pour the chocolate sauce into a small dish, if desired.

24 mini chocolate cupcakes baked in white paper liners

1 can (16 ounces) vanilla frosting

48 caramels (Kraft), unwrapped

24 $^3/_8$-by-2$^1/_2$-inch slips of paper with printed fortunes (make your own on a computer or write them by hand and cut them to size)

Orange candy fruit slices (optional)

1. Spread the tops of the cupcakes with the vanilla frosting and smooth.

2. For the cookies, microwave several caramels at a time for 2 to 3 seconds to soften slightly. Press 2 caramels together and roll out to an approximately 3-inch round. Cut out a 3-inch circle using clean scissors, a cookie cutter, or the rim of a glass. Repeat with the remaining caramels. Place a paper message down the center of a caramel circle, allowing it to overhang one side. Fold the opposite sides of the round up over the message to enclose it in a half-moon shape. Bring the ends together to make a fortune-cookie shape.

3. Place the caramel fortune cookies on top of the cupcakes, pressing down lightly to adhere and place the orange candy fruit slices on the side, if using.

BANANA SPLIT

The inside scoop on this split is that anisette cookies dipped in melted yellow frosting and placed end to end make the banana. The ice cream is frosting tinted to look like vanilla, strawberry, and chocolate. The cherries are shaped from red fruit chews and have licorice lace for stems.

12 **vanilla cupcakes baked in white paper liners**

1 **can (16 ounces) plus 1 cup vanilla frosting**

3 **tablespoons low-sugar strawberry preserves (Smucker's)**

1 **cup canned chocolate frosting**

Yellow food coloring

8 **anisette cookies (Stella D'oro Anisette Toast)**

1 **red licorice lace**

12 **red fruit chews (Jolly Rancher, Starburst)**

12 **thin pretzel sticks (Bachman)**

¹/₂ **cup hot fudge sauce, plus extra for serving**

1 **cup whipped topping (Cool Whip)**

Coarse white decorating sugar for sundae dish (Cake Mate; optional)

2 **tablespoons chocolate sprinkles**

1. Divide the can of vanilla frosting evenly between two bowls. Mix the strawberry preserves into one bowl of frosting until well blended. Spoon the chocolate frosting into another bowl. Freeze all three bowls of frosting until firm, about 30 minutes. Tint the remaining 1 cup vanilla frosting pale yellow with the yellow food coloring. Spoon the yellow frosting into a microwavable measuring cup.

2. Place a wire rack over a cookie sheet. Microwave the yellow frosting, stopping to stir frequently, until it has the texture of lightly whipped cream, 30 to 35

Banana splits served in sundae dishes turn any occasion into a party. Add a pitcher of fudge sauce on the side for all your chocoholic friends.

seconds. Dip an anisette toast into the melted frosting, tipping the measuring cup to cover the toast almost completely. Pull the toast out of the frosting and allow the excess frosting to drain back into the cup. Place the dipped toast on the wire rack, flat side down. Repeat with the remaining toasts. Refrigerate until set, about 20 minutes.

3. For the cherry stems, cut the red licorice lace into six 2-inch pieces. Cut each piece in half lengthwise. For the cherries, microwave several red fruit chews for 2 to 3 seconds. Shape each fruit chew into a ball. Use a toothpick to score one side of the fruit chew to shape the cherry and to make a hole in the top. Repeat with the remaining fruit chews. Insert a pretzel stick into the base of each cherry for support (see page 19). Insert a piece of trimmed licorice into the hole on the top of the cherry. Spoon the fudge sauce into a ziplock bag. Spoon the whipped topping into a ziplock bag. Press out the excess air and seal the bags. Refrigerate the whipped topping until ready to serve.

4. For the vanilla ice cream, scoop the chilled vanilla frosting into small pieces, using an ice cream scoop or a large spoon. Place the frosting pieces, overlapping slightly, on top of 4 of the cupcakes to look like a scoop of ice cream. Repeat with the chocolate and the strawberry frostings on top of the remaining 8 cupcakes.

5. Sprinkle four sundae dishes with the white decorating sugar, if desired. Arrange 3 cupcakes, one of each flavor, in each sundae dish. When ready to serve, snip a 1/4-inch corner from the bag with the fudge sauce and pipe a small amount on top of the vanilla scoop. Snip a 1/2-inch corner from the bag with the whipped topping and pipe a dollop of whipped topping on top of each scoop. Sprinkle the tops with the chocolate sprinkles. Insert the cherry candies, pretzel stem down and licorice lace up, into the scoops. Arrange 2 dipped anisette toasts behind the scoops in each dish to make the banana. Serve with extra fudge sauce.

THE COALS ARE READY

The secret to perfect grilling is the charcoal, and ours is red hot and ready to glow. Orange sprinkles and Oreo cookie crumbs create the sparks, and our fresh ground USDA chuck patties are made from popcorn cakes with a little red food color spray.

12 chocolate or vanilla cupcakes baked in brown paper liners (see Sources)

COALS

1 bag (10 ounces) marshmallows

1 can (16 ounces) vanilla frosting

Black food coloring (McCormick)

2 tablespoons orange sprinkles (Cake Mate)

1 cup ground chocolate cookies (Oreos, Famous Chocolate Wafers)

1 tablespoon confectioners' sugar

BURGERS

4 caramel popcorn cakes (Quaker Oats)

1 can (1.5 ounces) red food color spray (Wilton, Cake Mate)

Clean small grill and clean grill rack (optional)

1. For the coals, using clean scissors, cut the marshmallows into halves and thirds. Attach the marshmallow pieces to the cupcakes, 4 to 5 per cupcake, with some of the vanilla frosting to secure. Place the cupcakes in the freezer until set, about 10 minutes.

2. Tint the remaining vanilla frosting light gray with the black food coloring. Microwave in a microwavable measuring cup, stopping to stir frequently, until it has the texture of lightly whipped cream, about 35 seconds. Holding 1 chilled cup-

cake by its paper bottom, dip it into the gray frosting just up to the paper liner. Allow the excess frosting to drip off back into the cup (see page 15). Turn right side up and transfer to a cookie sheet. While the frosting is still wet, sprinkle the top with a few orange sprinkles. Repeat with the remaining cupcakes and sprinkles. If the frosting becomes too thick for dipping, reheat for several seconds in the microwave, stirring well.

3. Transfer the cupcakes to a serving platter or the grill, if using. Sprinkle the area around and in between the marshmallows with the chocolate cookie crumbs. Dust the tops with the confectioners' sugar.

4. For the burgers, spray the tops and sides of the popcorn cakes with the red food color to cover. Arrange them on a platter or the grill rack, if using, to look like burgers ready to grill.

BAKE-SALE PIES

CUPCAKE

Our berry pie cupcakes are as easy as . . . pie! The blueberry and cherry filling is blue or red candies, and the frosting is tinted to look like a lattice crust. At your next bake sale, cover the table with these mini pastries, and we promise you will sell out!

24 vanilla cupcakes baked in silver foil liners (Reynolds)

2 cans (16 ounces each) vanilla frosting

  Yellow food coloring

1 teaspoon unsweetened cocoa powder

1 cup each red and blue candy (My M&M's, Jelly Belly)

1. Tint the vanilla frosting with 3 or 4 drops of the yellow food coloring and the cocoa powder to make a light brown for the piecrust. Spread some of the frosting on top of a cupcake, leaving $1/4$ inch of the cupcake edge exposed. For the filling, arrange about 25 like-colored candies close together on top of the cupcake. Repeat with the remaining cupcakes and like-colored candies.

2. Spoon the remaining light brown frosting into a ziplock bag, press out the excess air, and seal. Snip a small ($1/8$-inch) corner from the bag. For the lattice crust, pipe 4 or 5 lines across the top of a cupcake, about $1/2$ inch apart. Pipe 4 or 5 more lines, on the diagonal. Pipe a beaded edge around the top of the cupcake (see page 13). Repeat with the remaining cupcakes and frosting.

3. Arrange the cupcakes on a wire rack and make several bake-sale tags to put with the cupcakes.

You Say It's Your Birthday?

Let's make it all about you. Whether it's bling, karaoke, painting, or crochet, birthdays make all your fixations seem okay. Robots, race cars, fuzzy monsters too. Go ahead, enjoy, it's all a part of you. Indulge a passion, fuel a fire, transform that obsession into the cupcake of your desire.

Ring Pop candy

Chiclets

decorating sugar

vanilla frosting

foil liner

colored paper

ring pop base

RING BLING

Mini cupcake jewelry made from Ring Pops will turn your little girl's party into the one not to miss. Set up gem stations where kids can choose from their favorite candies and sparkling sugars to create their own Ring Bling cupcakes. For even bigger bling, try the finger plate variation that can hold a whopping 24 carats of candy.

24 **mini vanilla cupcakes baked in gold or silver liners (see Sources)**

24 **Ring Pops or 24 Fingerfood party plates for the ring bases (see Sources)**

Colored decorating sugars (Cake Mate)

1 **can (16 ounces) plus 1 cup vanilla frosting**

Assorted candies (M&M's Minis, Chiclets Tiny Size gum, Jujubes, Tootsie Pop Drops, and spice drops, if using Fingerfood party plates)

3/4 **cup white chocolate chips**

Colored paper, cut into 3-inch scalloped circles (Marvy paper punch; see Sources)

1. If using Ring Pops for the base, remove the hard candies from the rings; set aside. Cut a small hole in the center of the colored paper circles and insert the plastic tip of the ring through the paper. Use a toothpick to poke a hole in the base of the cupcake liners.

2. Place each colored sugar into a small shallow bowl. Spread the tops of the mini cupcakes with the vanilla frosting and smooth. Arrange candies on top as desired to make the ring design, leaving the center open for the large gemstone from the Ring Pop. Roll the top of the cupcake in the desired colored sugar. Press the Ring Pop gemstone into the center of the cupcake. Repeat with the remaining cupcakes, candies, and sugars.

3. Place the white chocolate chips in a ziplock bag; do not seal. Microwave for about 10 seconds to soften. Massage the mixture and return to the microwave. Repeat the process until the chocolate is smooth, about 1 minute total (see page 18). Press out the excess air. Snip a small (1/8-inch) corner from the bag. Pipe a dot of melted white chocolate on the plastic tip of each ring before adding the cupcake. Use a small juice glass to hold the Ring Pop ring upright and refrigerate until set, about 5 minutes.

4. If using Fingerfood party plates, roll out a few spice drops on a lightly sugared work surface to a 1/8-inch thickness. Cut into small shapes using scissors or small cookie cutters; set aside. Place each colored sugar into a small shallow bowl. Spread the top of a mini cupcake with the vanilla frosting and smooth. Arrange candies and some of the cut spice drops on top of the cupcake as the ring design. Roll the top of the cupcake in the desired colored sugar. Repeat with the remaining cupcakes, candies, and sugars.

5. Spoon the remaining vanilla frosting into a ziplock bag, press out the excess air, and seal. Snip a small (1/8-inch) corner from the bag and pipe lines and dots of frosting along the outer edge of the plates, adding sugar or remaining candies as desired (leave the center of the plate open for the cupcake).

6. Place the white chocolate chips in a ziplock bag; do not seal. Microwave for about 10 seconds to soften. Massage the mixture and return to the microwave. Repeat the process until the chocolate is smooth, about 1 minute total (see page 18). Press out the excess air. Snip a small (1/8-inch) corner from the bag and pipe a dot of chocolate in the center of the Fingerfood plate. Place the bottom of the decorated cupcake into the chocolate, pressing to secure. Use a small juice glass to hold the Fingerfood plate upright and refrigerate until set, about 5 minutes.

FUR BALLS AND STRING MONSTERS

ez CUPCAKE

It was a mosh, yes, a monster mosh. It was so simple, we were done in a flash. We used a Dum Dum, a sour fruit ring, M&M eyes, and a mini cupcake thing. Frosting turned green, orange, purple too. We created a monster, so frightening and new. Go grab some candy, a cupcake or two, and in no time at all, you'll be doing it too.

12 **vanilla cupcakes baked in orange, green, and purple paper liners (see Sources)**

12 **mini vanilla cupcakes, paper liners removed**

1 **can (16 ounces) vanilla frosting**

Neon green, orange, and purple food coloring (see Sources)

24 **mini lollipops (Dum Dums), unwrapped**

24 **peach or green apple gummy rings (O's)**

24 **brown mini candy-coated chocolates (M&M's Minis)**

12 **assorted color candy-coated chocolates (M&M's Minis)**

1. Spoon 2 tablespoons vanilla frosting into a small ziplock bag. Divide the remaining vanilla frosting among three bowls and tint each a different color with the food coloring. Spoon each color of frosting into a separate ziplock bag, press out the excess air, and seal the bags.

2. Insert a lollipop stick through a gummy ring, pushing it through the candy from the center to outer edge. Bring the gummy ring up around the lollypop, like a bonnet, to make the eyes. Continue with the remaining gummy rings and lollipops.

3. Snip a small (¹/₈-inch) corner from the bags with the frostings. Pipe a dot of tinted frosting on top of the standard cupcakes. Place a mini cupcake on top, flat side down. Starting at the edge of the standard cupcake and using the tinted frosting, pipe fur with a squeeze-release-pull action (see page 13). Continue until the entire exposed cupcake assembly is covered. Repeat with the remaining cupcakes and colored frosting.

4. Insert 2 like-colored lollipop eyes into the top of each cupcake assembly. Pipe a dot of vanilla frosting in the center of each lollipop and add a brown candy for the pupil. Add a colored candy to the top of the frosting for the nose. Repeat with the remaining lollipop eyes and cupcakes.

VARIATION: String monsters: Follow steps 1 and 2. Snip a small (¹/₈-inch) corner from the bags with the frosting. Pipe a dot of tinted frosting on top of the standard cupcakes. Place a mini cupcake on top, flat side down. Pipe the tinted frosting all over the cupcakes to make the string, making sure to cover cupcakes completely. Continue with step 4.

FORMULA ONE CUPCAKES

Preheat your ovens, and sort your candies. Our Formula One race car has oversize doughnut tires, a chocolate spoiler and straight pipes, and a shiny red-sugar-coated paint job. Drivers, start your engines!

19 **vanilla cupcakes baked in red paper liners (see Sources)**

1 **can (16 ounces) plus 1 cup vanilla frosting**

Red and black food coloring (Wilton)

1 **cup canned dark chocolate frosting**

1 **cup dark cocoa candy melting wafers (Wilton)**

2 **vanilla wafers**

1 **thin pretzel stick (Bachman)**

1 **graham cracker**

1 **cup red decorating sugar (Cake Mate)**

2 **yellow and 4 white candies (Mentos)**

2 **chocolate-frosted doughnuts**

2 **mini chocolate-frosted doughnuts**

2 **chocolate sticks (Hershey's)**

1. Spoon $^1/_4$ cup vanilla frosting into a ziplock bag, press out the excess air, seal, and set aside. Tint the remaining vanilla frosting red with the red food coloring, cover, and set aside. Tint the dark chocolate frosting black with the black food coloring. Spoon the black frosting into a ziplock bag, press out the air, seal, and set aside.

2. Place the dark cocoa candy melting wafers in a ziplock bag; do not seal. Microwave for 10 seconds, massage the bag, and repeat the process until smooth, about 45 seconds total (see page 18). Press out the excess air and seal. Place the templates (page 61 and 62) on a cookie sheet and cover with wax paper. Snip a small ($^1/_8$-inch) corner from the bag and pipe the outline of the spoiler and

racing numbers, then fill in with the melted candy. Tap the pan lightly to smooth the surface. Repeat, using the templates, to make the roll bar, straight pipes, steering wheel, and exhaust pipe parts. Refrigerate until set, about 5 minutes.

3. Pipe a dot of the melted candy onto the flat side of 1 vanilla wafer. Place the end of the pretzel stick into the melted candy to cover (see page 19). To make the driver's head, sandwich the remaining vanilla wafer, flat side down, on top, pressing into the melted candy. Place on the cookie sheet and refrigerate until set, about 5 minutes.

4. Cut the graham cracker with a serrated knife crosswise into 4 equal pieces. Trim $1/4$ inch lengthwise from 2 of the pieces. Place the red sugar in a small bowl. Spread a very thin layer of the red frosting on top of the graham cracker pieces. Invert the pieces into the red sugar and press lightly to coat. Transfer the pieces, sugar side up, to a cookie sheet.

5. Reserve $1/3$ cup of the red frosting in a small bowl. Spread the remaining red frosting on top of 15 of the cupcakes and smooth. Starting on the edge, roll the cupcakes in the red sugar to cover completely (see page 17).

6. Heat the reserved $1/3$ cup red frosting in the microwave for about 5 seconds, stir well, and heat again to get the consistency of slightly whipped cream. Dip one side of the cookie head into the frosting to cover. Dip the other side halfway into the frosting to make the top of the helmet. Allow the excess frosting to drip off back into the bowl (see page 15). Transfer to a wax paper–lined cookie sheet, half-dipped side up. Refrigerate for 15 minutes.

7. Snip a very small ($1/16$-inch) corner from the bags with the vanilla and black frosting. Pipe the mouth and goggles on the racer's face with the black frosting. Pipe a dot of black frosting on one edge of 2 red-sugared cupcakes. Attach a yellow candy to each frosting dot as the headlight. Pipe crosshatch lines on the yellow candies with the black frosting to make the light guards. Snip a larger opening from the bag with the black frosting and pipe frosting on top of the 4 unfrosted cupcakes. Spread the frosting to the edge and smooth. For the front and rear tires, press a chocolate doughnut, flat side down, on top of each of the 4 cupcakes.

8. Arrange the cupcakes on a serving platter or cutting board in the shape of the race car (see the photo on page 59): 1 red cupcake in front, a row of the 2 red

cupcakes with the headlights, a row of 3 made up of the 2 mini-doughnut cup-cakes on their sides as the front wheels and 1 red cupcake in the center, a row of 3 red cupcakes, a row of 3 made up of the 2 doughnut cupcakes on their sides as the rear wheels with 1 red cupcake in the center and the center cup-cake topped with another red cupcake, and a last row of 3 red cupcakes with another row of 3 red cupcakes on top.

9. Cut one of the chocolate sticks in half crosswise. Insert each cut piece of choco-late into the outer cupcakes in the last row. Pipe a dot of black frosting on the end of each chocolate stick. Carefully peel the chocolate spoiler from the wax paper and attach to the chocolate sticks, with the longer side facing out. Pipe a decorative edge around the wheels with the black frosting to fill the gap at the cupcake and attach the sugared graham cracker pieces to the frosting to make fenders; put the larger pieces on top of the larger doughnuts. Pipe 2 white lines

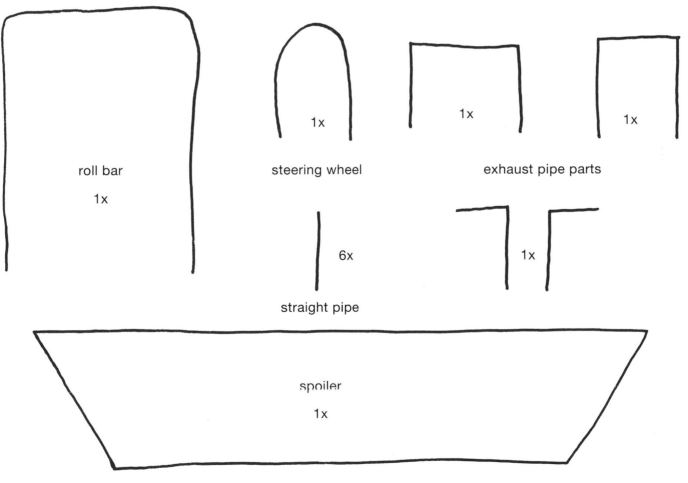

roll bar

1x

steering wheel

1x

exhaust pipe parts

1x   1x

straight pipe

6x   1x

spoiler

1x

of frosting on top of the helmet and insert the head, pretzel stick down, into the center cupcake as the driver. Place the remaining chocolate stick down the center front of the car and pipe a white line down either side of the chocolate stick using the vanilla frosting. Carefully peel the numbers, roll bar, straight pipes, steering wheel, and exhaust pipe parts from the wax paper and place on the cupcakes as shown in the photograph. Pipe black frosting into the opening of each doughnut wheel and add the white candies as the hubcaps.

FLOWER POWER

Please *do* eat the daisies—and the daffodils and posies too. Each blossom in our garden of candy delights is built on a cookie, with melted white chocolate holding the petals in place. Pretzel supports keep our garden standing tall (see the photo on page 3).

 6 vanilla cupcakes baked in green paper liners (see Sources)

1/4 cup yellow decorating sugar (Cake Mate)

 3 tablespoons pink or light pink decorating sugar (Cake Mate)

 3 marshmallows

20 mini marshmallows

 2 thin chocolate cookies (Famous Chocolate Wafers)

 7 vanilla wafers

 5 mini vanilla wafers

1/2 cup white chocolate chips (Nestlé)

 6 orange candies (Runts)

30–33 small red jelly beans (Jelly Belly)

 3 yellow cereal O's (Froot Loops)

 4 spice drops (orange, red, and yellow)

25 orange candy-coated chocolates (M&M's)

 5 green mini candy-coated chocolates (M&M's Minis)

24 thin pretzel sticks (Bachman)

 5 candy spearmint leaves (Farley's)

 1 cup flaked sweetened coconut

   Yellow and green food coloring

 1 cup canned vanilla frosting

 1 cup small green jelly beans (optional; Jelly Belly)

1. Place the yellow and pink decorating sugars in separate small shallow bowls. Using scissors, cut the standard marshmallows crosswise into 5 pieces, allowing the pieces to fall into the yellow sugar. Shake the bowl, tossing the marshmallow pieces to coat with the sugar. Cut the mini marshmallows on the diagonal and let them fall into the pink sugar bowl. Toss the pieces with the sugar until coated.

2. Arrange like cookies close together on a large cookie sheet. Place the white chocolate chips in a ziplock bag. Do not seal the bag. Microwave for 10 seconds to soften. Massage the chips in the bag, return to the microwave, and repeat the process until the chocolate is smooth, about 1 minute total (see page 18). Press out the excess air and seal.

3. Snip a very small (1/16-inch) corner from the bag with the chocolate. For the yellow flowers, pipe a circle of melted chocolate 1/2 inch from the edge of the chocolate wafers and another small circle in the center. Add the yellow sugared marshmallow pieces, overlapping them slightly along the outer edge, and 3 orange candies in the center. For the red flowers, pipe white chocolate in a circle along the edge of 3 of the standard vanilla wafers. Attach the red jelly beans along the edge, side by side and radiating out from the center. Pipe a dot of white chocolate in the center and add a yellow cereal O. For the pink flowers, pipe white chocolate in a circle along the edge of the 4 remaining standard vanilla wafers. Attach the pink sugared marshmallows side by side, pointed ends radiating out. Flatten the spice drops slightly. Pipe a dot of white chocolate in the center of the vanilla

wafers and add a spice drop. For the orange flowers, pipe some white chocolate on the flat side of the mini vanilla wafers. Arrange 5 orange candy-coated chocolates on top, close to the edge. Add the mini green candies in the center. Place all of the cookie flowers in the refrigerator until set, about 5 minutes.

4. Remove the cookie flowers from the refrigerator and turn over. Pipe a line of white chocolate on the center of each cookie, reheating the chocolate in the microwave for several seconds to soften if necessary. Place the end of a pretzel stick into the chocolate on each cookie and turn to coat (see page 19). Refrigerate until set, about 5 minutes.

5. Place the spearmint leaves flat side down. Cut the leaves in half horizontally so they are thin. Insert a pretzel stick into the wide end to make 10 leaves.

6. Place the coconut in a ziplock bag. Add a few drops of yellow and 1 drop of green food coloring. Massage the bag with the coconut until completely tinted (see page 16). Pour the coconut into a shallow bowl. Tint the vanilla frosting light green with the green and yellow food coloring. Spread the green frosting on top of the cupcakes and smooth. Roll the edges of the cupcakes in the coconut (see page 17).

7. Arrange the cupcakes close together in a shallow dish. Sprinkle some of the green jelly beans in the open areas. Just before serving, insert the pretzel ends of the flowers into the cupcakes, trimming the pretzel sticks as necessary to make a full bouquet. Add the spearmint leaves.

KARAOKE CUPCAKES

CUPCAKE

These cupcakes will inspire your inner idol with miniature microphones made from an ice cream cone and a doughnut hole coated with silver sprinkles. There's a licorice remote antenna at the base of the cone, so rock out and conquer the stage.

24 **vanilla cupcakes baked in silver foil liners (Reynolds)**

 1 **can (16 ounces) plus 1 cup vanilla frosting**
   Red food coloring

24 **mini kids' ice cream cones (Joy)**

24 **pieces pink licorice pastels (Jelly Belly)**

24 **plain doughnut holes**

 1 **cup mini silver dragées (see Sources) or decorating sugar or sprinkles**

1. Tint the can of vanilla frosting light pink with a few drops of red food coloring. Cover and set aside. Spoon ¼ cup of the remaining frosting into a small ziplock bag, press out the air, seal, and set aside.

2. For the antenna, use a wooden skewer or toothpick to make a small hole in the base of each cone. Snip a small (⅛-inch) corner from the bag with the vanilla frosting and pipe a small dot of frosting into the hole. Insert a pink licorice pastel halfway into each hole. Pipe a line of vanilla frosting around the top inside edge of each cone. Press a doughnut hole into the opening of the cone.

3. Place the silver dragées (or decorating sugar or sprinkles) in a small bowl. Gently spread a thin layer of the remaining ¾ cup vanilla frosting over a doughnut hole. Press the frosting into the dragées to cover the doughnut hole completely. Repeat with the remaining doughnut holes.

4. Spread the tops of the cupcakes with the pink frosting and smooth. Place the cone microphones on top of the cupcakes, pressing down to secure.

ARTIST'S PALETTE

What's our favorite canvas? Cupcakes, of course! Tint frosting to make the paint colors and sculpt a brush from Tootsie Rolls and a bread stick.

7 vanilla cupcakes, 1 in each of the following paper liners: yellow, orange, red, pink, purple, blue, and green (see Sources)

3 chocolate chews (Tootsie Rolls)

1 can (16 ounces) vanilla frosting

1 plain bread stick, 6 inches long

1 3-inch piece strawberry fruit leather (Fruit by the Foot)

Yellow, orange, red, purple, blue, and green food coloring

Painter's palette (optional; can be cut from a piece of cardboard or found at arts and crafts stores; see Sources)

1. For the bristles of the paintbrush, microwave the chocolate chews for no more than 3 seconds on high. Press the candies together and roll out on a clean work surface into a 1/8-inch-thick rectangle about 21/2 by 4 inches. Use scissors to cut the rectangle crosswise, almost all the way through, every scant 1/8 inch; it will look like fringe. Place a dot of frosting 1/2 inch from one end of the bread stick. Place the uncut side of the rolled-out chocolate chew against the frosted end of the bread stick and roll it around the bread stick to make the brush. Place the fruit leather overlapping the chocolate and the bread stick and roll it around the bread stick, ending with a dot of water to secure. Loosen the chocolate fringe and lightly press the ends together to make a paintbrush; set aside.

2. Divide the frosting evenly among seven small bowls. Make sure to keep the bowls covered with plastic wrap to prevent the top from drying. Tint each bowl of frosting a different color with the food colors. (Use the red food coloring to make one bowl of red frosting and one bowl of pink.)

3. Matching the frosting color to the color of the paper liners, spread an even layer of frosting over the cupcakes.

4. Arrange the cupcakes on a painter's palette, if desired, and add the paintbrush.

KNIT ONE, FROST TWO

Every knitter will want a skein of these cupcakes. Are you a crocheter? Leave the candy off the top of the bread stick and cut a notch near the tip to make a crochet needle that won't drop a stitch.

12 vanilla cupcakes baked in white paper liners

¹/₂ cup white chocolate chips (Nestlé)

6 wheat sticks (Pringles or Milk Pocky)

6 pale yellow large candy sprinkles (Wilton, Smarties)

1 can (16 ounces) plus 1 cup vanilla frosting

Neon blue and neon pink food coloring (McCormick)

6 blue and 6 pink candy melting wafers (Wilton)

Garnish: Paper label (4 by 8 inches)

1. For the knitting needles, line a cookie sheet with wax paper. Place the white chocolate chips in a microwavable 1-cup measuring cup, microwave for 10 seconds, stir, and repeat until the chocolate is smooth, about 45 seconds total. Hold the end of a wheat stick, tip the measuring cup, and dip into the chocolate to cover almost completely. Allow the excess chocolate to drip off back into the cup. Transfer to the wax paper. Repeat with the remaining wheat sticks. Refrigerate for 5 minutes, or until set.

2. Reheat the chocolate for several seconds if necessary. Peel the chilled dipped wheat sticks from the wax paper. Redip the chocolate end about ¹/₈ inch deep into the chocolate and attach the flat sprinkle or Smartie to make the knitting needles. Return to the cookie sheet, propping the wheat stick on the edge of the pan, and refrigerate until set, about 5 minutes.

3. Divide the frosting in half. Tint one part neon blue and one part neon pink with the food coloring. Spread a generous mound of blue frosting on top of 6 of the cupcakes. Press a blue candy wafer, flat side up, in the center of each mound. Spoon the remaining blue frosting into a ziplock bag, press out the excess air,

seal, and snip a small (¹/₈-inch) corner from the bag. For the yarn, pipe alternating lines of frosting to cover the mound, but not the center candy wafer. Repeat with the remaining 5 cupcakes. Follow the same directions for the pink frosting and pink candy wafers.

4. Insert 2 of the cookie knitting needles candy end up into 3 of the cupcakes, avoiding the candy melt at the center. To make a skein of yarn, place 2 like-colored cupcakes on their sides on a serving platter. Wrap the paper label around the cupcakes. Surround with blue and pink cupcake balls of yarn and needles.

MAKING WAVES

Whether you're heading down the rapids, diving in the surf, or planning a party at the wave pool, these big splashy cupcakes will keep things cool. Our vanilla wafer family paddles up a storm with their fruit chew flippers. And while the kids are over their heads in white water, Mom and Dad float along on chocolate doughnut inner tubes. Someone throw the kids a Life Saver!

8 **vanilla cupcakes baked in blue paper liners (see Sources)**

6 **mini vanilla cupcakes baked in white paper liners**

2 **pink fruit chews (Jolly Rancher, Starburst, Laffy Taffy)**

1 **yellow and 1 green fruit chew (Laffy Taffy)**

3 **tablespoons granulated sugar**

7 **candy spearmint leaves (Farley's)**

5 **red gumdrops (Dots)**

1 **green gumdrop (Dots)**

9 **mini vanilla wafers**

1 **can (16 ounces) plus 1 cup vanilla frosting**

   Yellow, red, and blue food coloring

$^{1}/_{4}$ **cup canned chocolate frosting**

4 **chocolate-frosted doughnuts**

$^{1}/_{2}$ **cup chocolate-covered assorted nuts (Brach's Bridge Mix)**

   Blue cellophane for serving (optional)

1. For the flippers, microwave the fruit chews for 2 to 3 seconds to soften. Roll out each fruit chew separately on a clean work surface to a $^{1}/_{8}$-inch thickness. Cut each fruit chew into two 1-by-2-inch triangles. For the zigzag ends of the flippers, use a pastry wheel or craft pinking scissors. Score one side of the fins

with the back of a small knife to make ridges. For the reeds, sprinkle the work surface with the sugar and roll out the spearmint leaves to a ¹/₈-inch thickness. Cut the flattened spearmint leaves with clean scissors into zigzag grass shapes. For the bikini top, trim ¹/₄ inch from the flat end of 2 of the red gumdrops. For the beer bottle, cut a green gumdrop in half lengthwise, then cut a notch from each side at the rounded end.

2. For the arms, using a serrated knife, cut ¹/₄ inch from each side of 3 of the mini vanilla wafers. For the torsos, cut ¹/₈ inch on a diagonal from each side on the top edge of 3 more mini vanilla wafers, creating a tapered point at the top (you may need to adjust the size of the vanilla wafer depending on the size of the opening on your doughnut).

3. Tint 2 tablespoons of the vanilla frosting yellow and 2 tablespoons red with the food coloring. Spoon each color frosting into a separate small ziplock bag. Spoon the chocolate frosting into a small ziplock bag. Press out the excess air from the bags and seal. Spoon the remaining vanilla frosting into a bowl, tint with the blue food coloring, and stir slightly, leaving some of the white frosting unincorporated for white streaks.

4. Spoon a dollop of the white-streaked blue frosting on top of a cupcake. Spread the frosting to cover the top of the cupcake. Using an offset spatula or the back of a spoon, gently pull the frosting in an upward motion to make spiky waves. Repeat to cover all of the cupcakes. For the inner tubes, arrange the chocolate doughnuts on top of 4 of the frosted standard cupcakes at different angles. Add some more blue frosting to create waves around the inner tubes. To some of the remaining standard and mini cupcakes, add the green spearmint reeds and use the chocolate-covered nuts as rocks, spacing them randomly on top of the remaining cupcakes. (Leave some of the cupcakes unadorned for the water.)

5. Place a torso vanilla wafer, pointed side up, in the center

of a doughnut. Snip a very small ($1/16$-inch) corner from the bags with the chocolate, red, and yellow frostings. Pipe a dot of chocolate frosting on each side of the torso vanilla wafer near the top. Attach the vanilla wafer arms, cut side toward the center, on either side of the torso. Place a red gumdrop, flat side down, above the torso to support the head, add a drop of frosting to the gumdrop, and place a whole vanilla wafer for the head on top of the gumdrop, letting it rest on the torso. Repeat with 2 more of the chocolate doughnut cupcakes. Using the chocolate, red, and yellow frostings, pipe hair and features on the 3 vanilla wafer faces and torsos. For the woman tuber, pipe red frosting lines for the bikini straps and attach the trimmed red gumdrops, cut side down, to the frosting lines. For the man tuber, add a dot of frosting and attach the bottle at the end of one arm. Insert flippers at the base of the 3 doughnuts with vanilla wafers and add 2 flippers upright in the center of the remaining cupcake inner tube, using frosting to secure.

6. Arrange the cupcakes on a blue platter or on top of some blue cellophane to look like water, if desired.

ROBOCUP

Under that shiny sci-fi veneer lies a tasty cyborg: half robot, all cupcake. Add a few gizmos and blinking lights made from colorful candies and frosting, and your Robocup is ready to roll.

18 **vanilla cupcakes baked in silver foil liners (Reynolds)**

1 **can (16 ounces) plus 1 cup vanilla frosting**

Black food coloring (McCormick)

5 **whole graham crackers**

1 **cup gray decorating sugar (see Sources)**

4 **plain bread sticks**

4 **thin wheat sticks (Pringles)**

3 **red and 4 white jelly rings (Chuckles)**

2 **vanilla wafers**

1 **tube (4.25 ounces) brown decorating icing (Cake Mate)**

16 **brown, 6 blue, 4 green, 4 yellow, and 2 orange mini candy-coated chocolates (M&M's Minis)**

6 **red, 2 blue, and 2 brown candy-coated chocolates (M&M's)**

5 **red and 1 white licorice pastels (Jelly Belly)**

1 **square candy-coated gum (Chiclets)**

1 **red gumdrop (Dots)**

1. Tint all of the vanilla frosting light gray with a few drops of the black food coloring. Spoon ³/₄ cup of the frosting into a ziplock bag, press out the air, seal, and set aside. Cover the remaining frosting with plastic wrap until ready to use.

2. For the head, using a serrated knife, trim 1 inch from one end of 1 whole graham cracker, reserving the trimmed piece for the mouth. Cut the remaining 4 whole graham crackers in half crosswise to make 8 square pieces. Set aside 4 squares for the chest. For the legs, cut 1 square in half to make 2 rectangles. For the arms and feet, cut 2 squares in half on a diagonal to make pieces that are 1 inch

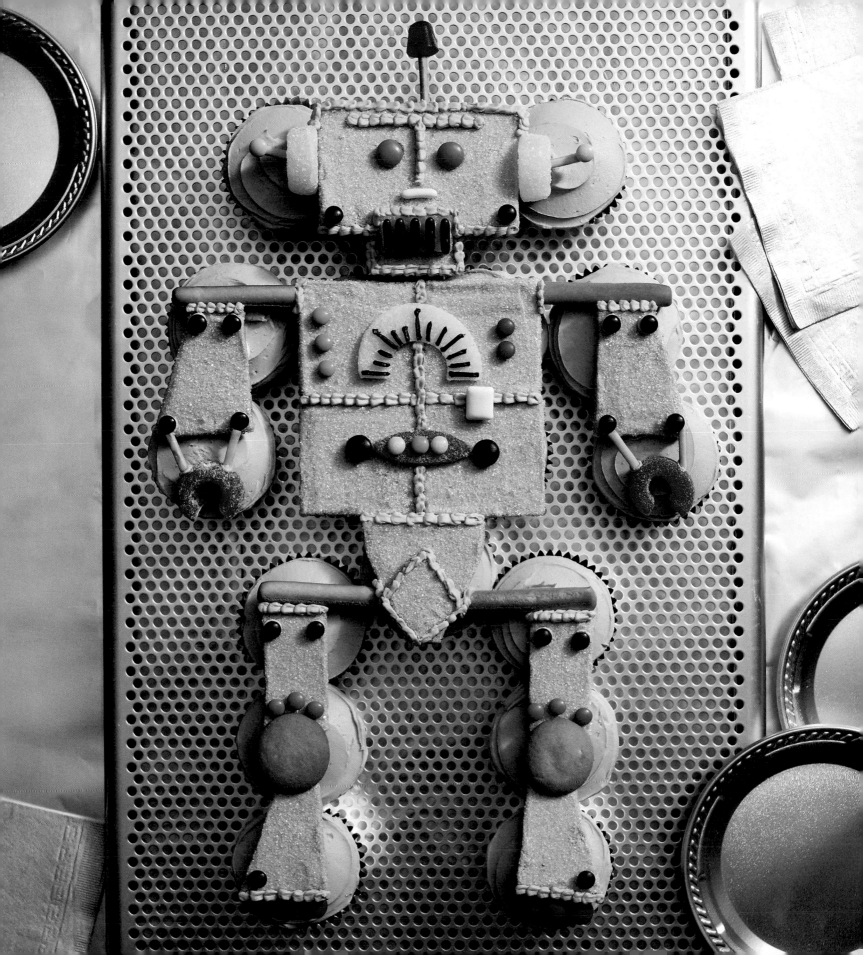

wide at the top and $1\frac{1}{4}$ inches wide at the bottom. For the pelvis, trim $\frac{3}{4}$ inch from 2 corners of 1 square. Put the sugar in a small shallow bowl.

3. Spread a very thin layer of the gray frosting on top of each graham cracker and smooth. Place a frosted cracker piece, frosted side down, into the sugar to cover. Transfer the sugar-coated cracker piece to a cookie sheet, sugared side up. Repeat with the remaining crackers and sugar.

4. Using a serrated knife, cut the plain bread sticks into four $2\frac{1}{2}$-inch pieces. Cut the thin wheat sticks into three 3-inch pieces and four 1-inch pieces. For the hands, remove one fourth of 2 red jelly rings. Press together the red jelly ring pieces and the remaining red jelly ring and roll out on a lightly sugared work surface to a $\frac{1}{8}$-inch thickness. To make the red control panel, use scissors to cut the sheet of rolled candy into a 1-by-$2\frac{1}{2}$-inch oval. Roll out 2 of the white jelly rings on a lightly sugared surface to a $\frac{1}{8}$-inch thickness. For the semicircular meter panel, cut a $2\frac{1}{2}$-inch circle from the flattened jelly rings. Cut a $1\frac{1}{4}$-inch hole in the center and cut the ring in half. Using the scraps, cut a $1\frac{1}{2}$-by-1-inch rectangle for the mouth.

5. Spread the remaining gray frosting on top of the cupcakes and smooth. Arrange the cupcakes on a serving platter in this order: 3 across for the head, leaving space between the head and chest, a square group of 4 for the chest, 2 lengthwise for each arm, leaving a space between the hands and the chest, 1 for the pelvis, and 3 lengthwise for each leg.

6. Snip a small ($\frac{1}{8}$-inch) corner from the bag with the gray frosting. Using the photo as a guide, arrange the sugared graham crackers, bread sticks, and vanilla wafers on top of the cupcakes, securing with dots of gray frosting. Make sure that the chest crackers line up evenly. Pipe beaded lines (see page 13) of gray frosting along the seams between the chest crackers. Add additional beaded lines to crackers and bread sticks.

7. Pipe dots of frosting and attach the 2 remaining white jelly rings to make the ears, the two trimmed red jelly rings for the hands, and the jelly shapes cut for the control panel, meter panel, and mouth. Using the brown icing, pipe lines on top of the meter panel. Using dots of gray frosting, attach the wheat sticks as the 4 hand extensions and 3 antennae, M&M's as the bolts, eyes, buttons, lights, and toes, licorice pastels as the mouth grill and nose, gum as the start button, and gumdrop as the antenna light.

JUNGLE FEVER

If those crocs and hippos get a taste of flamingo, they are in for a real treat, because the flavor is a subtle mix of pink jelly bean, banana Runt, pink chocolate, and pretzel. The crocs and hippos don't taste bad either, since they are made from Nutter Butter cookies and Froot Loops.

HIPPOS

 4 **vanilla cupcakes baked in blue paper liners (see Sources)**

¹/₃ **cup blue decorating sugar (Cake Mate)**

 1 **cup canned vanilla frosting**

 Neon blue food coloring (McCormick)

 4 **peanut butter sandwich cookies (Nutter Butter)**

 8 **mini chocolate chips**

16 **pieces orange cereal O's (Froot Loops)**

1. Place the blue sugar in a small shallow bowl.

2. Spoon 2 tablespoons of the vanilla frosting into a small ziplock bag, press out the excess air, seal, and set aside. Tint the remaining vanilla frosting blue with the food coloring. Spread the blue frosting on top of the cupcakes and smooth. Roll the edge of the cupcakes in the sugar (see page 17).

3. For the hippo heads, press a cookie into the frosting of each cupcake, allowing one third of the cookie to hang over the edge. Snip a small (¹/₈-inch) corner from the bag with the vanilla frosting. Pipe dots of the frosting onto the peanut butter cookie for the eyes, nostrils, and ears. Attach the chocolate chips, flat side up, to the frosting to make the eyes and attach the cereal pieces to make the ears and nose.

FLAMINGOS

12 mini vanilla cupcakes baked in white paper liners

1 cup pink candy melting wafers (Wilton)

12 thin pretzel sticks (Bachman)

12 large pink jelly beans

6 banana-shaped candies (Runts), halved crosswise

1/2 cup pink decorating sugar (Cake Mate)

1 cup canned vanilla frosting

Black food coloring (McCormick)

1. Line a cookie sheet with wax paper. Place the pink candy melting wafers in a 1-cup glass measuring cup. Microwave for 10 seconds to soften, stir, return to the microwave, and repeat until the candy is smooth, about 1 minute total.

2. For the necks and heads, hold the end of a pretzel stick and tip the measuring cup; dip the stick into the melted candy to cover almost completely. Allow the excess candy to drip off back into the cup. Transfer the coated pretzel stick to the wax paper. Dip one end of a jelly bean into the melted candy and attach to the coated end of the pretzel at an angle to make the head. Repeat with the remaining pretzels and jelly beans. For the beaks, dip the cut ends of the halved banana candies into the melted candy. Attach to the other end of the jelly bean to make the beak (see the photo above). Refrigerate until set, about 5 minutes.

3. Spoon the remaining melted candy into a small ziplock bag; do not seal the bag. Reheat in the microwave for 5 to 10 seconds if necessary. Press out the excess air and seal. Place the wing templates (page 81) on a cookie sheet and cover with wax paper. Snip a small ($^{1}/_{8}$-inch) corner from the bag and pipe the outline of the wings, then fill in with melted candy. Tap the pan lightly to smooth surface. Repeat to make 12 sets of wings. Refrigerate until set, about 5 minutes.

4. Place the pink sugar in a small shallow bowl. Tint 1 tablespoon of the vanilla frosting black with the food coloring. Spoon into a ziplock bag, press out the excess air, seal, and set aside. Spread the remaining vanilla frosting on top of the mini cupcakes, mounding it slightly in the center. Starting on the edge, roll the cupcakes in the pink sugar to cover completely (see page 17).

5. Gently peel the chilled flamingo head assemblies and wings from the wax paper. Insert the pretzel stick all the way into each cupcake close to one side. Press the wings into each cupcake on either side of the neck. Snip a very small ($^{1}/_{16}$-inch) corner from the bag with the black frosting and pipe dots of frosting for the eyes and a line on the banana candy to mark the tip of the beak.

CROCODILES

4 vanilla cupcakes baked in blue paper liners (see Sources)

1 cup canned vanilla frosting

Black and neon blue food coloring (McCormick)

$^{1}/_{3}$ cup each blue and green decorating sugar (Cake Mate)

4 peanut butter sandwich cookies (Nutter Butter)

8 pieces green cereal O's (Froot Loops)

1. Tint 2 tablespoons of the vanilla frosting black with the food coloring. Spoon the black frosting into a ziplock bag, press out the excess air, seal, and set aside. Spoon $^{1}/_{4}$ cup of the vanilla frosting into a ziplock bag, press out the excess air, seal, and set aside. Tint the remaining vanilla frosting blue with the food coloring.

2. Place the blue sugar in a small shallow bowl. Spread the blue frosting on top of the cupcakes. Roll the edge of the cupcakes in the sugar (see page 17).

3. For the croc heads, trim the edges of the cookies with a serrated knife to form a

long V-shape. Place the green sugar in a shallow bowl. Snip a small (¹⁄₈-inch) corner from the bag with the vanilla frosting and pipe on top of the trimmed cookies to cover; spread smooth. Press the frosted side of the cookies into the green sugar and cover completely. Attach the sugared cookies to the frosted cupcakes, sugar side up, allowing one third of the cookie to hang over the edge.

4. For the eyes, trim the bottom edge of the green cereal pieces. Pipe 2 dots of vanilla frosting at the back of the head and attach the trimmed pieces of cereal, cut side down. Pipe teeth on the outer edges of the heads with the remaining vanilla frosting in the bag, starting at the top edge of the cookie and using the squeeze-release-pull technique (see page 13) to make sharp teeth. Snip a small (¹⁄₈-inch) corner from the bag with the black frosting and pipe dots to make the nostrils and eyes.

REEDS

12 mini vanilla cupcakes baked in blue paper liners (see Sources)

¹⁄₄ cup granulated sugar

5 candy spearmint leaves (Farley's)

¹⁄₂ cup canned vanilla frosting

Neon blue food coloring (McCormick)

¹⁄₄ cup blue decorating sugar (Cake Mate)

1. Sprinkle the granulated sugar on a clean work surface. Roll out the spearmint leaves to a scant ¹⁄₄-inch thickness, using additional sugar as necessary to prevent sticking. For the reeds, cut the flattened candies into zigzag grass shapes with clean scissors.

2. Tint the vanilla frosting blue with the food coloring. Spread the blue frosting on top of the mini cupcakes. Place the blue decorating sugar in a small shallow bowl and roll the edge of the cupcakes in the sugar (see page 17). Insert several pieces of the cut spearmint leaves into the frosting as reeds.

3. Arrange the cupcakes on tiered cake stands, with the flamingos above and the hippos and crocs lurking below. Fill in with reeds as desired.

I Thought You Ordered Chocolate Moose

Critters made from candy and cupcakes, what a pair, almonds used as wings, frosting for hair. Circus peanuts for fins, breakfast treats for tails, Twinkies and chocolate wafers for whales. Cookies for hounds' ears and honeycomb too, cherry fruit slices for lobster—what a zoo!

candy melting wafers

Tootsie Roll

M&M's Minis

chocolate-covered sunflower seeds

Twinkie

frosting

CHOCOLATE MOOSE

Moose have a reputation for being a little ornery, but under the chocolate coating, this one is just a big Twinkie. I'm sure glad we didn't ask for the baked Alaska.

10 **chocolate cupcakes baked in silver foil liners (Reynolds)**

1¹/₂ **cups dark cocoa candy melting wafers (Wilton)**

10 **creme-filled snack cakes (Twinkies)**

1 **can (16 ounces) plus 1 cup chocolate frosting**

5 **chocolate chews (Tootsie Rolls)**

20 **brown candy-coated chocolate-covered sunflower seeds (Sunny Seed Drops)**

1 **tube (4.25 ounces) white decorating icing (Cake Mate)**

20 **brown mini candy-coated chocolates (M&M's Minis)**

White decorating sugar for serving dishes (see Sources)

1. Place the antler templates (page 88) on a cookie sheet and cover with wax paper.

2. Place the candy melting wafers in a ziplock bag; do not seal. Microwave for 10 seconds to soften. Massage them and return to the microwave. Repeat the process until the candy is smooth, about 60 seconds total (see page 18). Press out the excess air and seal the bag.

3. Snip a small (¹/₈-inch) corner from the bag and pipe the outline of an antler (see page 18). Fill in the antler with melted candy and tap the cookie sheet lightly to smooth the surface. Repeat to make 11 sets of antlers (the extra set is in case of breakage). Refrigerate until set, about 5 minutes.

4. Place a snack cake on its side, flat side facing you, and while holding your knife at an 11 o'clock angle, cut 2 inches off the left bottom corner (keep the larger right side to make the moose). Repeat with the remaining snack cakes.

5. Spread some of the chocolate frosting on top of the cupcakes. Press a trimmed snack cake, cut side down, into the frosting on each cupcake to secure (see photo above). Fill in the gaps at the base of the snack cake with frosting to smooth. Freeze the cupcakes until just firm, 15 to 20 minutes.

6. For the ears, cut the chocolate chews into quarters. Roll or press each piece into a 1/2-by-1-inch oval, shape one end into a point, and pinch the opposite end. Spoon 1/2 cup of the remaining chocolate frosting into a ziplock bag, press out the excess air, and seal.

7. Microwave the remaining chocolate frosting in a microwavable 2-cup measuring cup, stopping to stir frequently, until it has the texture of lightly whipped cream,

25 to 35 seconds. Holding a chilled cupcake by the foil liner, dip it into the chocolate frosting up to the liner. Allow the excess frosting to drip off back into the cup (see page 15). Turn right side up, tap the bottom of the cupcake lightly to flatten the frosting, and let stand. If the frosting begins to thicken while you are dipping, reheat it in the microwave for several seconds, stirring well. Allow the cupcakes to dry completely before decorating, about 30 minutes.

8. Carefully peel the chocolate antlers from the wax paper. Insert a set of antlers near the top edge of a cupcake at a slight angle. Snip a small ($\frac{1}{8}$-inch) corner from the bag with the chocolate frosting. Pipe dots of the chocolate frosting on the tip of the muzzle and attach the sunflower seeds as the nostrils. Pipe a mouth, beard, and tufts of fur between the antlers with the chocolate frosting. Poke a small hole with a toothpick in front of each antler and insert the chocolate ears, pinched end in. Pipe a dot of white icing on either side of the snack cake in front of the ears and attach the mini chocolates as the eyes. Pipe a small white highlight on each eye. Repeat with the remaining cupcakes.

9. Place each cupcake in a dish and fill the dish with white decorating sugar to keep the cupcake balanced.

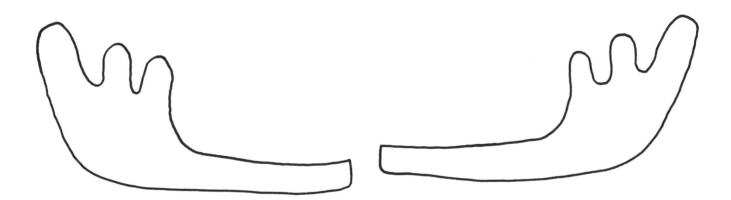

HOUND DOGS

You ain't nothin' but a . . . dachshund, four cupcakes long, dipped in melted frosting, with M&M eyes watching over a bone. And those custom cookie ears, snouts, and tails leave us all shook up.

8 chocolate cupcakes baked in brown paper liners (see Sources)

1/2 recipe cookie dough from Chocolate Sugar Cookies (page 225)

1 cup canned chocolate frosting

1 tube (4.25 ounces) each brown and white decorating icing (Cake Mate)

4 brown candy-coated chocolates (M&M's)

2 black jelly beans

8 chocolate-covered almonds

1/2 cup oat cereal O's (Cheerios; optional)

Dog bone–shaped graham cracker (Scooby-Doo Graham Cracker Stick or cut from cookie dough above; optional)

1. Preheat the oven to 350°F and line a cookie sheet with parchment paper.

2. Using the templates on page 91, cut out the faces, ears, and tails from the rolled-out cookie dough, following the directions on page 20. Bake until the cookies are firm to the touch and fragrant, 8 to 10 minutes. Transfer to a wire rack and cool completely.

3. Spoon the chocolate frosting into a shallow microwavable bowl. Heat the frosting in the microwave, stopping to stir frequently, until it has the texture of lightly whipped cream, 10 to 15 seconds.

4. Holding a cupcake by its paper liner, dip it into the frosting just up to the edge of the liner. Allow the excess frosting to drip off back into the bowl (see page 15). Carefully invert the cupcake and place on a cookie sheet. Repeat with the remaining cupcakes. If the frosting becomes too thick, microwave for several seconds, and stir.

5. Arrange 4 cupcakes in a row on a serving platter. Attach the head cookie and the ears and tail, securing them with a few dots of the brown decorating icing. Pipe several dots of brown icing and attach the brown candies for the eyes and a black jelly bean for the nose. Pipe a few lines of the brown icing for eyebrows. Pipe a white highlight on each eye with the white icing. Arrange the chocolate-covered almonds as the paws along the base of the cupcakes. Repeat with the remaining 4 cupcakes. Use the cereal as dog food and give your dog a bone, if desired.

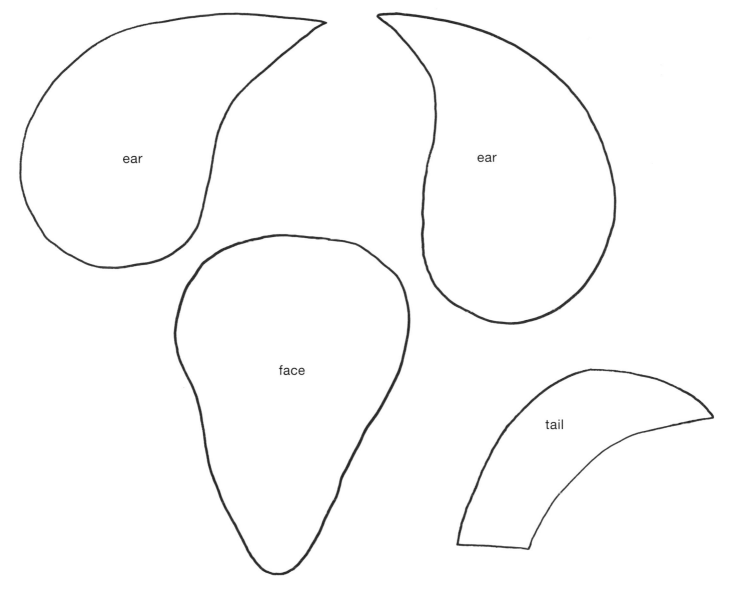

A TAIL OF TWO CRITTERS

Same tail—different ending. Both of our furry forest friends flaunt fluffy tails crafted from S-shaped breakfast treat cookies coated in melted frosting. Then each gets its unique look with marshmallow ears dipped in sugar for the squirrel and M&M ears and frosting fur for the skunk.

COOKIE TAILS

Follow these instructions and frost according to the critter recipe.

8 S-shaped breakfast treat cookies (Stella D'oro, or use ¹/₂ recipe cookie dough from Quick Sugar Cookies on page 225)

¹/₂ cup white or semisweet chocolate chips

16 thin pretzel or wheat sticks (Pringles)

1. Using a serrated knife, trim 1 inch on a diagonal from one end of each cookie to remove the curl. (See the photo on page 19; alternatively, using the template at right, cut cookies from the rolled-out cookie dough following the directions on page 20.)

2. Preheat the oven to 350°F and line a cookie sheet with parchment paper. Bake until firm to the touch and lightly golden, 7 to 12 minutes. Transfer to a wire rack and cool completely.

3. Place the chocolate chips in a ziplock bag; do not seal. Microwave for 10 seconds, massage the bag, and repeat until the chocolate is melted, about 30 seconds total (see page 18). Press out the excess air and seal.

4. Line a cookie sheet with wax paper. Place the cookies on the cookie sheet, flat side up. Snip a small (¹/₈-inch) corner from the bag of melted chocolate. Pipe a large dollop of chocolate on the flat side of each cookie near the cut or smaller end. Place 2 pretzel or wheat sticks into the chocolate to overhang the end by 2 inches, and turn to coat (see page 19). Refrigerate until set, about 5 minutes.

4 vanilla cupcakes baked in white paper liners

4 mini vanilla cupcakes baked in white paper liners

1 can (16 ounces) vanilla frosting

Black food coloring (McCormick)

$^1/_3$ cup white decorating sugar (see Sources)

1 tablespoon light pink decorating sugar (Cake Mate)

4 cookie tails (see page 92)

8 mini marshmallows

2 brown jelly beans

8 brown mini candy-coated chocolates (M&M's Minis)

1 tube (4.25 ounces) black decorating icing (Cake Mate)

1. Spoon $^1/_4$ cup of the vanilla frosting into a ziplock bag, press out the excess air, and seal. Tint the remaining vanilla frosting gray with the black food coloring.

2. Place the white and pink decorating sugars in separate shallow bowls. Spread the tops of the 4 standard cupcakes with some of the gray frosting and smooth. Roll the edges of the cupcakes in the white sugar (see page 17). Spoon $^1/_2$ cup of the gray frosting into a small microwavable bowl. Spoon the remaining gray frosting into a ziplock bag, press out the excess air, and seal.

3. Place the cookie tails, pretzel side down, on a wire rack over a wax paper–lined cookie sheet. Microwave the gray frosting in the bowl for about 5 seconds, until it has the texture of lightly whipped cream. Pour the gray frosting over the cookie tails to coat completely. Transfer the tails to the refrigerator until ready to decorate.

4. For the muzzles, cut 4 of the marshmallows on the diagonal to remove one third of the marshmallow. The larger pieces are for the muzzles. For the noses, cut the brown jelly beans in half crosswise. For the ears, use scissors to cut the remaining 4 marshmallows in half on the diagonal. Press the cut sides into the pink sugar to coat.

5. Snip a small ($^1/_8$-inch) corner from the bags with the vanilla and gray frostings. Pipe a small dot of the gray frosting on the lower half of a mini cupcake. Attach

the marshmallow muzzle, flat side against the cupcake and cut side toward the bottom edge. Pipe enough gray frosting on top of the mini cupcake to cover. Spread the gray frosting to cover the cupcake and marshmallow and smooth.

6. Roll the edge of the mini cupcake in the white sugar. Add the cut marshmallow ears, sugared side facing out, at the opposite edge from the muzzle. Pipe gray frosting on each ear to cover the unsugared area of the marshmallow. Add the chocolate candies as the eyes on either side of the muzzle and a piece of jelly bean, cut side down, as the nose. Pipe eyelids and a few whiskers with the gray frosting. Pipe a mouth with the black decorating icing. Repeat with the remaining mini cupcakes.

7. Turn the decorated head on its side and place on a standard cupcake, using a dot of frosting to secure if necessary. Pipe vanilla frosting as fur under the muzzle on both cupcakes. Refrigerate until you are ready to add the tails.

8. Place the cookie tails on a cookie sheet, pretzel side down. Starting at the curled end of the tail, pipe a line of gray frosting down the center of each tail and a few tufts of fur along the edge.

9. When ready to serve, insert the cookie tail's pretzel sticks into the standard cupcake, behind the head. Add a dot of frosting to the back of the mini cupcake head and press the tail into the dot to secure. Repeat with the remaining cupcakes.

ACORNS

1 tube (4.25 ounces) chocolate decorating icing (Cake Mate)

24 mini vanilla wafers

24 teardrop-shaped chocolates (Hershey's Kisses)

TO MAKE THE ACORNS: Pipe a dot of the chocolate decorating icing on the flat side of each vanilla wafer. Attach the flat side of a chocolate kiss to the icing. Pipe a dot of chocolate icing on top of the cookie as the stem.

4 vanilla cupcakes baked in brown paper liners (see Sources)

4 mini vanilla cupcakes baked in brown paper liners (see Sources)

$^1/_2$ cup canned vanilla frosting

1 can (16 ounces) dark chocolate frosting

Black paste food coloring (Wilton)

$^1/_3$ cup black decorating sugar (see Sources)

4 cookie tails (see page 92)

4 mini marshmallows

2 light pink jelly beans

8 brown candy-coated chocolates (M&M's)

1 tube (4.25 ounces) chocolate decorating icing

1. Spoon the vanilla frosting into a ziplock bag, press out the excess air, and seal. Tint the chocolate frosting black with the black food coloring.

2. Using the black sugar in place of the white sugar (disregard the pink sugar) and the black frosting in place of the gray, follow instructions in step 2 for the squirrels.

3. Using the microwavable bowl of black frosting, follow instructions in step 3 for coating the squirrel tails (don't worry about covering all of the edges of the cookies for the skunk tails).

4. Using the 4 mini marshmallows and the pink jelly beans in place of the brown jelly beans, follow instructions in step 4 for the squirrels' muzzles and noses (disregard the instructions for the ears).

5. Using the black frosting in place of the gray, follow instructions in step 5 for the squirrels for attaching the marshmallow muzzles and frosting the mini cupcake heads.

6. Pipe 2 dots of black frosting on opposite sides near the top of the mini cupcake and attach the brown candies as the ears. Pipe several lines of black frosting

around the outside of the ears to cover the edges. Starting under the marshmallow muzzle, pipe $\frac{1}{2}$-inch strokes of black frosting along the edge of the cupcake, working your way around the cupcake, always pulling the frosting away from the center (see page 13). Continue piping to completely cover the cupcake and muzzle, slightly overlapping the rows. Starting between the ears, pipe short lines of vanilla frosting along the center of the cupcake and muzzle, always pulling up, to make the white stripe. Attach a piece of jelly bean, cut side down, as the nose at the tip of the muzzle. Pipe the eyes with the chocolate decorating icing. Repeat with the remaining mini cupcakes.

7. To attach the heads, follow instructions in step 7 for the squirrels.

8. Place the cookie tails on a cookie sheet, pretzel side down. Starting at the curled end of each tail, pipe several rows of vanilla frosting $\frac{1}{2}$ inch from the edge, overlapping slightly and pulling the frosting away from the center, to make an outline of the tail. Repeat with black frosting along the outside edge.

9. To attach the tails, follow instructions in step 9 for the squirrels.

KOI POND

Koi goldfish made from circus peanuts transform a simple platter of cupcakes into a golden pond. The fish float on overlapping blue and white paper bubbles for a very coy look.

24 vanilla cupcakes baked in blue paper liners (see Sources)

1 can (16 ounces) plus ¹/₂ cup vanilla frosting

Blue food coloring

48 orange circus peanuts

48 orange peanut butter–filled candy-coated chocolates (Peanut Butter M&M's)

24 orange cereal O's (Froot Loops, Apple Jacks)

48 brown mini candy-coated chocolates (M&M's Minis)

White and blue paper circles (optional)

White and light blue candy-coated chocolates for serving (My M&M's; optional)

1. Spoon ¹/₂ cup of the vanilla frosting into a small ziplock bag, press out the excess air, seal, and set aside. Tint the remaining can of vanilla frosting pale blue with a few drops of the blue food coloring. Cover and set aside.

2. For the fins, place 24 of the circus peanuts on their sides and cut lengthwise into 2 slices, to make 48 slices. Lay each slice cut side down and cut each in half on the diagonal to make 96 pieces. For the bodies, place the remaining 24 circus peanuts flat side down and make a diagonal cut from one end, removing no more than ¹/₄ inch (see photo, page 101).

3. Spread the tops of the cupcakes with the light blue frosting and smooth. Place 1 of the circus peanut bodies on top of each frosted cupcake. Arrange fins, cut side up and pointed ends out, 2 at the uncut end of each circus peanut body and 2 on either side in the middle.

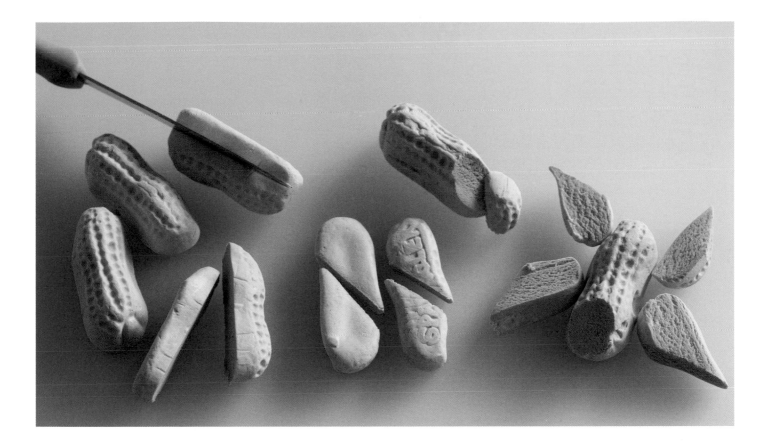

4. Snip a small (¹/₈-inch) corner from the bag with the vanilla frosting. Pipe a large dot of frosting at the cut end of the circus peanut body. Press 2 orange candies into the dot of frosting for the eyes and 1 cereal O for the mouth. Pipe small dots of vanilla frosting on the orange candies and add the brown candies for the pupils. Repeat on all of the koi bodies with the remaining frosting and candies.

5. If you like, arrange the cupcakes on a surface with circles cut from white and blue papers and sprinkle the platter with white and light blue candies.

RED LOBSTER CUPCAKES

Seafood for the cupcake lover in you. We rolled cherry fruit slices in sugar to make sheets out of the candy and cut them to make the pieces for the shell. Our lobster is served up on a tasty bed of cookie crumbs (the sand) and has red licorice antennae and legs.

23 vanilla cupcakes, 9 baked in red paper liners (optional; see Sources) and 14 baked in white paper liners

1 cup granulated sugar

4 bags (10 ounces each) cherry candy fruit slices

20 candy spearmint leaves (Farley's)

1¹/₂ cups graham cracker crumbs

1 can (16 ounces) plus 1 cup vanilla frosting

Red food coloring

2 red licorice laces

2 black licorice pastels (Jelly Belly)

8 red licorice twists (Twizzlers)

Green licorice laces

5 lemon candy fruit slices

1. Sprinkle a clean work surface with some of the sugar. Working with 3 cherry fruit slices at a time, press together and roll out on the sugared surface to a ¹/₈-inch thickness, adding more sugar as necessary to prevent sticking. Cut out the template shapes (see page 104) using a paring knife or clean scissors. Repeat with all of the cherry fruit slices, incorporating any scraps as you go and adding more sugar as necessary, to make 1 head, 2 large claws, 2 small claws, 13 small shell pieces, and 18 large shell pieces. For the seaweed, roll out the spearmint leaves in the sugar to a ¹/₈-inch thickness, then pinch on one side.

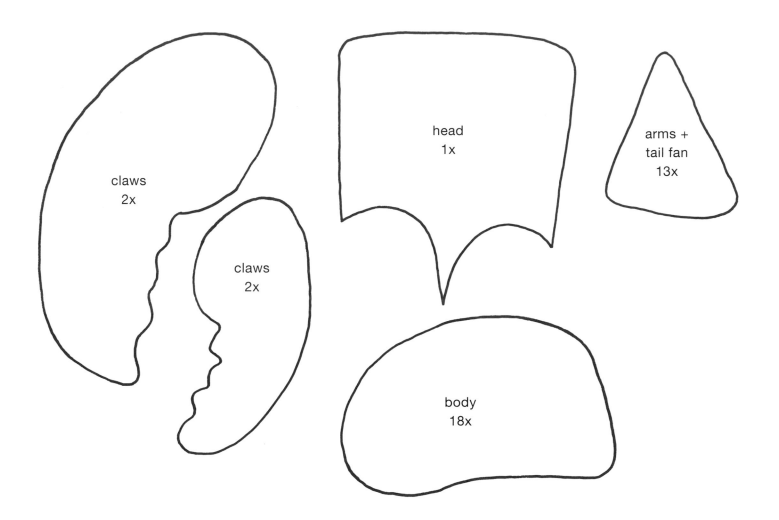

2. Place the graham cracker crumbs in a shallow bowl. Spoon 1 tablespoon vanilla frosting into a small ziplock bag, press out the excess air, seal, and set aside. Tint 1 cup of the vanilla frosting red with the food coloring. Spread 9 cupcakes (the ones with the red paper liners if using) with the red frosting. Spread the vanilla frosting on the remaining 14 cupcakes. Roll the tops of the vanilla-frosted cupcakes in the graham cracker crumbs to cover completely (see page 17).

3. Arrange the cupcakes on a serving platter, placing 5 crumb cupcakes for each arm and claw, 1 for the head, 3 rows of 2 red cupcakes side by side for the body, 3 red cupcakes for the tail, and the remaining 3 crumb cupcakes for the fan of the tail (see photo on page 103 for arrangement).

4. Using the cherry fruit pieces and starting at the fan of the tail, place 7 small shell pieces overlapping slightly on the 3 crumb-coated cupcakes. Arrange 2 large shell pieces on each red tail cupcake, overlapping as you work your way up the tail toward the body. Continue with the 6 red body cupcakes, placing 2 large shell pieces on each and overlapping as you go. Place the head piece on the crumb-coated head cupcake. For the claws, place 3 small shell pieces in a row and place large and small claw pieces at the end, placing the large claw pieces toward the outside.

5. Snip a small (1/8-inch) corner from the bag with the vanilla frosting and pipe dots along the inside edges of the lobster claws. Insert the red licorice laces into the head cupcake as the antennae and add the black licorice pastels as the eyes. Cut the red licorice twists into eight 4-inch and eight 2-inch pieces. For the feelers, press the longer pieces along the body. Add the smaller pieces on the ends. For the seaweed, place the pinched spearmint leaves and green licorice laces around the lobster on the platter. Garnish with the lemon fruit slices.

WHALE OF A GOOD TIME

Save the whales, eat more Twinkies. These frosting-coated snack cake denizens of the deep dive in and out of cupcakes topped with wavy frosting, while marshmallow seagulls perched on cookie pilings keep watch for landlubbers.

12 vanilla cupcakes baked in blue paper liners (see Sources)

4 creme-filled snack cakes (Twinkies)

2 thin chocolate cookies (Famous Chocolate Wafers)

2 cans (16 ounces each) vanilla frosting

Black, yellow, and blue food coloring (McCormick)

1 chocolate creme-filled rolled wafer cookie (Pepperidge Farm Pirouette)

1 yellow licorice lace

2 marshmallows

4 mini marshmallows

4 yellow candy-coated chocolate-covered sunflower seeds (Sunny Seed Drops)

White, blue, and light blue candy-coated chocolates (My M&M's)

1. Place a snack cake on its side, flat side facing you, and holding a knife at an 11 o'clock angle, cut in half on the diagonal (see photo, page 108). One half will have the rounded side up when placed cut side down on the cupcake; reserve this piece for the head. For the tail, place the other half on the work surface, flat side up, and trim a 1½-inch-long wedge from each side of the rounded end (see photo). Repeat with the remaining 3 snack cakes; you will have 4 heads and 4 tails. Using a serrated knife, cut the chocolate cookies in half. Cut a ¼-inch notch in the center of each straight side of the cut cookies.

2. Spread some of the vanilla frosting on top of 8 of the cupcakes. Press 1 head or tail cake piece, flat cut side down, into the frosting on each cupcake. Using

a paring knife, cut a horizontal slit in each of the tail end pieces and insert a chocolate cookie half, with the notch facing out (see photo at right), using some vanilla frosting to secure. Freeze the cupcakes until just firm, about 20 minutes.

3. Tint 1½ cups of the vanilla frosting light gray using the black food coloring. Spoon the gray frosting into a 2-cup microwavable measuring cup and microwave, stopping to stir frequently, until it has the texture of lightly whipped cream, 20 to 30 seconds. Remove 1 cupcake from the freezer at a time. Holding the cupcake by its paper bottom, dip it into the gray frosting to coat the snack cake and tail completely. Allow the excess frosting to drip off back into the cup (see page 15). Turn right side up and let stand. Repeat with the remaining cupcakes. If the frosting becomes too thick, reheat for several seconds, stirring well.

4. Tint ¼ cup of the remaining gray frosting black with the black food coloring. Spoon into a ziplock bag, press out the excess air, seal, and place in the refrigerator to firm, about 10 minutes.

5. Tint 1 tablespoon of the vanilla frosting yellow with the yellow food coloring. Spoon into a ziplock bag, press out the excess air, and seal. Divide the remaining 1 cup vanilla frosting into thirds. Using the blue food coloring, tint one part of the frosting light blue and one part of the frosting dark blue. Leave the remaining third white. Spoon each color into a separate ziplock bag, press out the excess air, and seal.

6. Snip a small (⅛-inch) corner from each bag of frosting. To create waves, pipe swirls using the light blue, dark blue, and white frosting on top of all 12 of the cupcakes (pipe one color on top of another to blend), swirling the frosting over the edges of the Twinkie whales.

7. For the pilings, cut the rolled wafer cookie crosswise into thirds. Insert the 3 cookie pieces in the center of one of the whaleless cupcakes, pushing them in to make staggered heights. Wrap the yellow licorice around the cookies and secure with a dot of yellow frosting.

8. For the seagulls' bodies, cut the standard marshmallows in half crosswise. Cut each half in half again crosswise to create 4 semicircles. For the seagulls' heads, attach a mini marshmallow on its side to one end of the straight side of each marshmallow semicircle. Using vanilla frosting to secure, attach 1 seagull on top of the cookie pilings. Press the remaining 3 seagulls into the frosting on top of the remaining cupcakes, leaving a couple of cupcakes with just waves. For the beaks, pipe a dot of yellow frosting on each head and secure the yellow sunflower seeds. Using black frosting, pipe the eyes and wings on the seagulls, and the eyes, mouths, and blowholes on the whales.

9. Place the cupcakes on a serving platter and sprinkle the blue and white candies around the bases of the cupcakes.

ANTS ON A PICNIC

CUPCAKE

The ants come marching one by one, but they leave paired with watermelon slices stacked on their M&M backs. We hear they can lift fruit slices twenty times their own weight on those frosting legs.

12 vanilla cupcakes baked in green paper liners (see Sources)

4 green and 4 red candy fruit slices

1 cup flaked sweetened coconut

Green and yellow food coloring

¹/₂ cup canned dark chocolate frosting

1 can (16 ounces) vanilla frosting

36 brown candy-coated chocolate-covered almonds (M&M's, Brach's Bridge Mix)

1. For the watermelon rind, use a 1¹/₂-inch round cookie cutter or a paring knife to cut out a semicircle from each green fruit slice; reserve the outside edge. For the watermelon flesh, repeat with the red fruit slices and reserve the center areas. Insert the insides from the red fruit slices into the outsides from the green fruit slices to make the watermelons. Cut ¹/₄ inch from the top straight edge through both the green and red pieces.

2. Pulse the coconut in a food processor until finely chopped. Transfer the coconut to a ziplock bag. Add 3 drops of green food coloring and 1 drop of yellow. Seal the bag and shake vigorously until the coconut is tinted grass green (see page 16). Place the coconut in a shallow bowl.

3. Spoon the dark chocolate frosting into a ziplock bag, press out the excess air, and seal.

4. Tint the vanilla frosting spring green with green food coloring and a few drops of yellow. Spread the top of a cupcake with the green frosting and smooth. Roll the edge of the cupcake in the coconut (see page 17). Repeat with the remaining cupcakes and frosting.

5. Snip a small (1/8-inch) corner from the bag with the chocolate frosting. Arrange 3 brown candies in a row on top of each cupcake, securing with a dot of chocolate frosting between the candies. Pipe 3 jointed legs on each side of each center candy (see "flying" straight lines, page 13). Pipe 2 chocolate antennae on each head. Pipe chocolate dots to look like seeds on the watermelon candies. Pipe a dot of chocolate frosting on the center candy of 4 of the ants and attach the watermelon slices. Arrange the cupcakes so the ants are marching in a row.

BUSY BEES

Let's get buzzy! We created a honeycomb from hexagonal cookies using custom-made cookie cutters, pressed the cookies into frosting, and filled the centers with honey. Our busy bees are made from black jelly beans, a drizzle of yellow frosting, and sliced almonds.

13 **vanilla cupcakes baked in yellow paper liners (see Sources)**

1/2 **recipe dough from Quick Sugar Cookies (page 225)**

1/2 **cup yellow decorating sugar (Cake Mate)**

3 **tablespoons light corn syrup**

1 **can (16 ounces) vanilla frosting**

Yellow and black food coloring

17 **large black jelly beans (Farley's)**

1/4 **cup sliced almonds (pick through to find the best shapes)**

3/4 **cup honey**

1. Preheat the oven to 350°F and line a cookie sheet with parchment paper.

2. Using a small paring knife or a homemade cookie cutter made from the larger template (page 115), cut the rolled-out dough into the larger honeycomb shapes (see the photo on page 114). Transfer the cutouts to the cookie sheet, about 1 inch apart. Cut out the centers of the honeycomb shapes with a small paring knife or a homemade cookie cutter made from the smaller template, remove the center dough from each, and reroll the scraps as necessary. Bake the cookies until firm to the touch and lightly golden, about 10 minutes. Transfer to a wire rack and cool completely.

3. Place the yellow sugar in a shallow bowl. Microwave the corn syrup in a microwavable bowl until boiling, 5 to 10 seconds. Brush the top of one of the cooled cookies with the corn syrup and dip into the yellow sugar to coat. (The cookies can be made up to 2 days in advance and kept in an airtight container.)

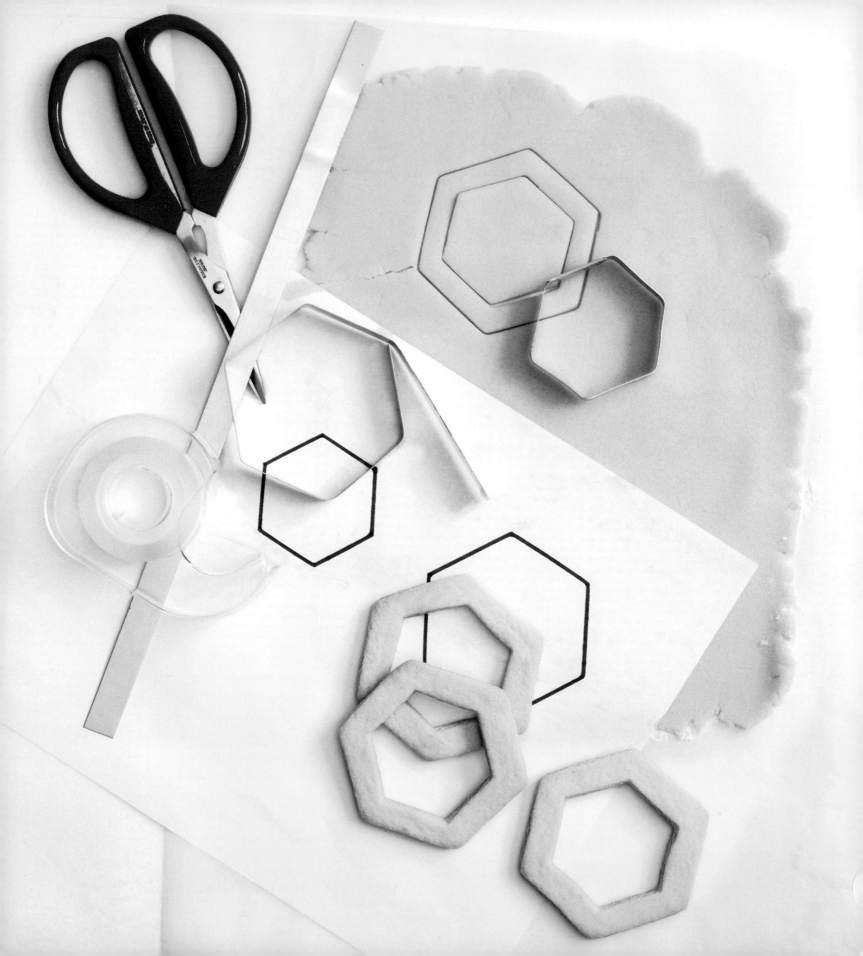

4. Tint ¼ cup of the vanilla frosting yellow and ¼ cup black with the food coloring. Spoon each color into a separate ziplock bag. Spread the tops of the cupcakes with the remaining vanilla frosting and smooth. Place the cookies on top of the cupcakes, sugared side up, pressing them into the frosting to seal any gaps.

5. Arrange 5 cupcakes on a serving platter in a center row, flat sides of the cookies touching. To create the honeycomb, place 4 cupcakes in rows on either side, positioning the cookies to fill in the gaps between the cupcakes in the center row. Level the cookies so they touch at the sides and check for gaps between cookies and frosting.

6. Snip a very small (¹/₁₆-inch) corner from the bags with the yellow and black frostings. For the bees, pipe 17 dots of black frosting randomly over the sugared cookies and attach the jelly beans. Pipe a zigzag line of yellow frosting on top of each jelly bean. Add 2 sliced almonds on each side of the jelly beans as wings, pressing them into the frosting to secure. Pipe a black dot of frosting for the head and a small pulled dot for the stinger (see page 13).

7. Just before serving, carefully spoon 2 to 3 teaspoons honey into the center of each honeycomb cookie to come up just to the cookie's edge. Serve immediately.

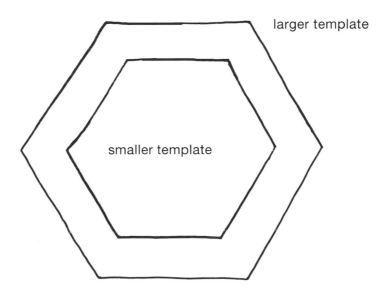

larger template

smaller template

Let's Party, Cupcake!

There's a pattern at this party: it's got apples for the teach, duckies for a baby shower, a sand castle for the beach. A shower of newborn babies, roses that are especially sweet, conversation hearts to break the ice, and Easter eggs that hide your treats. Coiffured grads, golf for the dads, a badminton birdie too. The pattern at this party is, there's a cupcake in it for you.

candy-coated
sunflower seeds

blue frosting

I'M SEEING A PATTERN

Whether your inspiration is a fabric, a wallpaper, or a party motif, find a pattern that interests you and study it for candy possibilities. Let your inner design guru lead you to a beautiful cupcake that celebrates your event. Follow the examples here or, better yet, find your own patterns to craft from candy.

FOR THE BLUE FLOWERS AND LEAVES: Frost the cupcakes with chocolate frosting. Tint vanilla frosting pale blue, place it in a ziplock bag, and follow the fabric for inspiration, piping the curving stems and leaves. Finally, add pale blue candy-coated chocolate-covered sunflower seeds and frosting to make the flowers.

FOR THE CHOCOLATE DOTS: Frost the cupcakes with a light tan frosting to match the fabric and place brown M&M's in diagonal rows to match the pattern.

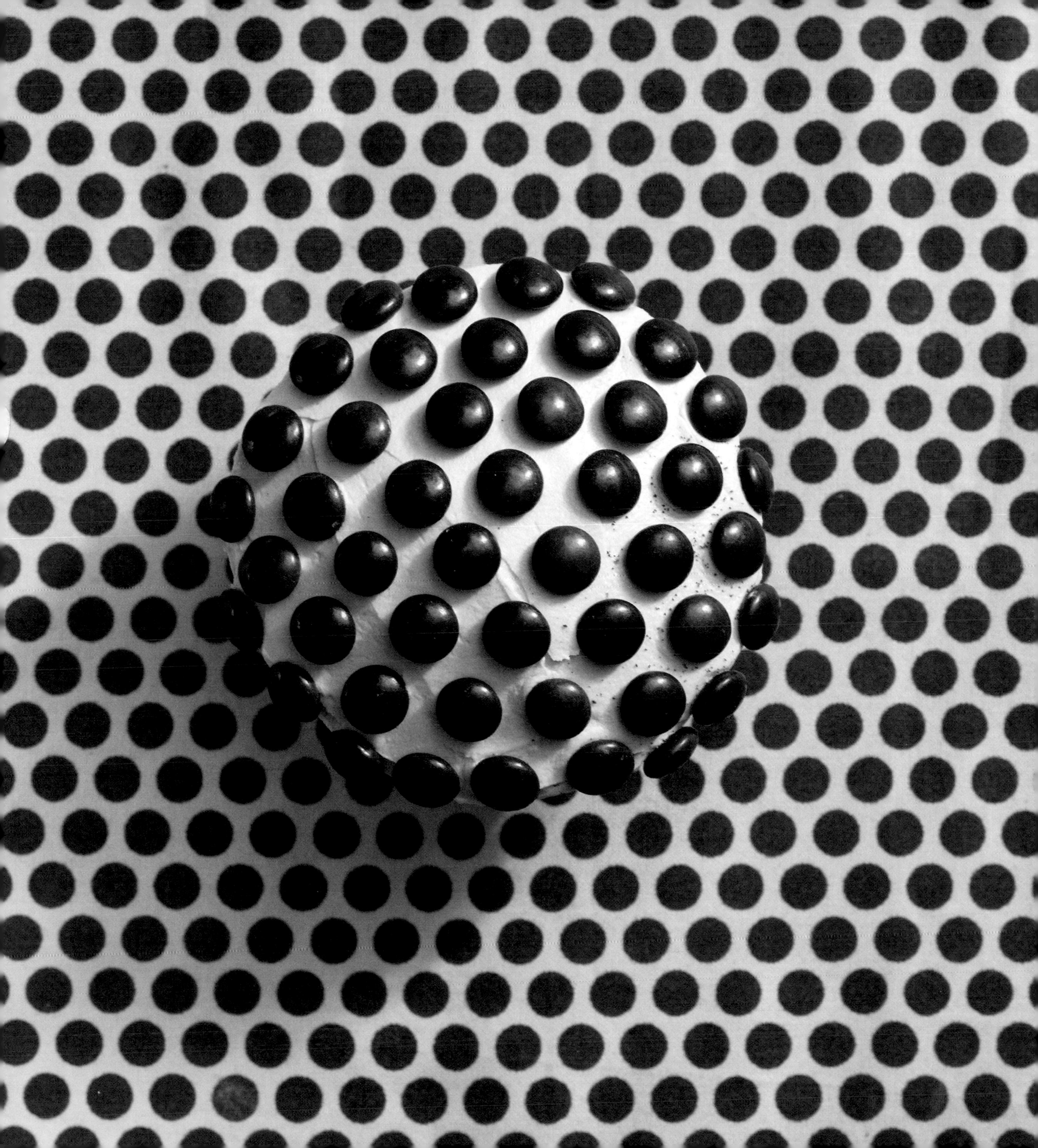

AN APPLE A DAY

Whether you want to put Snow White to sleep, butter up the teacher, keep the doctor away, or tempt Adam's fate, our apples will do the trick. They're made from doughnuts coated in red frosting, rolled in red sugar, and adorned with Tootsie Roll stems and fruit chew leaves.

8 **vanilla cupcakes baked in red paper liners (see Sources)**

1 **can (16 ounces) vanilla frosting**

   Red paste food coloring (Wilton)

8 **mini plain or chocolate-covered doughnuts**

4 **chocolate chews (Tootsie Rolls)**

6 **green fruit chews (Jolly Rancher, Tootsie Fruit Rolls)**

1 **cup red decorating sugar (Cake Mate)**

3 **black candy-coated chocolate-covered sunflower seeds (Sunny Seed Drops)**

1. Spoon 1 tablespoon of the vanilla frosting into a small ziplock bag, press out the excess air, and seal. Tint the remaining vanilla frosting red with the food coloring. Cut 1/2 inch from the bottom of each mini doughnut with a serrated knife and discard the bottom piece. Spread some red frosting on the cupcakes and place the mini doughnut piece, cut side down, on top (see photo, page 122). Place the cupcakes in the freezer for 10 minutes, or until slightly frozen.

2. For the stems, cut the chocolate chews in half lengthwise on the diagonal and shape each half into a stem (you will need 7). For the leaves, roll out the green fruit chews to a 1/8-inch thickness, and then cut into twelve 3/4-by-1 1/2-inch leaf shapes. Make a crease down the center of each leaf with the back of a paring knife and pinch one end.

3. Place the red decorating sugar in a medium shallow bowl. Working on 1 cupcake at a time, spread some of the red frosting on the top and sides of the doughnut and cupcake to fill in the gaps and lightly coat, making the doughnut top look like the top of an apple. Roll the frosted cupcake in the red sugar to coat (see page 17). Repeat with the remaining cupcakes.

4. To create a bite mark, carefully remove a 1½-inch-diameter divot in the side of 1 sugar-coated doughnut, using the tines of a fork or a paring knife. Snip a small (⅛-inch) corner from the bag with the vanilla frosting and pipe a thin layer of frosting to cover the exposed area inside the divot. Spread lightly with the back of a small spoon to smooth. Arrange the sunflower seeds in the vanilla frosting as the apple seeds, pointed ends toward the center. Insert the chocolate chew stems with the green fruit chew leaves at the top of the apple cupcakes. Arrange the cupcakes in a basket.

A ROSE IS A ROSE

By any other name, our roses would smell as sweet . . . as fruit slices. This romantic idea will win more hearts than memorizing all the sonnets of Shakespeare. When the flowers are presented in a box made for long-stems, it won't take an English professor to interpret the underlying theme: I love you.

19 **vanilla cupcakes, 12 baked in red paper liners and 7 baked in green paper liners (see Sources)**

1 **cup granulated sugar**

2 **bags (10 ounces each) cherry candy fruit slices**

6 **green fruit chews (Tootsie Fruit Rolls, Jolly Rancher)**

1 **cup red decorating sugar (Cake Mate)**

$1/2$ **cup white decorating sugar (see Sources)**

1 **can (16 ounces) vanilla frosting**

$1^1/2$ **cups small light green jelly beans (Jelly Belly)**

Long-stemmed rose box with tissue paper, ribbon, and note card (optional)

1. Sprinkle a clean work surface with some of the granulated sugar. Place a cherry fruit slice on the surface, sprinkle with additional granulated sugar, and roll out the candy to make a rough rectangle about $1/8$ inch thick, sprinkling with more sugar as necessary to prevent sticking (see photo, page 125). Repeat with the remaining fruit slices and granulated sugar.

2. For the roses, use scissors to cut the rolled-out candies in half lengthwise. Roll up 1 piece from a short end, jelly roll–style, to make the center of the rose (see page 125). Pinch the bottom edge. Add another strip of candy, continuing to roll up around the outside of the center, always pinching the bottom end to secure. Use 2 to 3 strips for each rose, loosening the roll to open the petals and create an open rose. Continue with the other fruit slices to make 12 roses, some

blooms larger than others (reserve a few of the candy petals for finishing). Set aside.

3. For the leaves, soften the green fruit chews in the microwave for 2 to 3 seconds. Roll out the fruit chews on a clean work surface to a ⅛-inch thickness. Cut the fruit chews into as many 1-inch-long leaf shapes as possible. Pinch one short end to give the leaf shape; set aside.

4. Place the red and white decorating sugars in separate shallow bowls. Spread the tops of the cupcakes with the vanilla frosting. Roll the edges of the cupcakes baked in the red paper liners in the red sugar (see page 17). Roll the edges of the cupcakes baked in the green paper liners in the white sugar.

5. Arrange 1 candy rose on top of each of the red-edged cupcakes. Add the reserved petals as necessary to finish the flowers. For the stems, add the green jelly beans, lengthwise in 3 rows, down the center of the white-edged cupcakes. Randomly arrange green fruit chew leaves on top of all of the cupcakes.

6. Line a platter or a long-stemmed rose box with tissue paper, if desired. Arrange a few of the rose cupcakes at one end. Add the stem cupcakes in a row, placing the jelly bean rows end to end. Add the remaining rose cupcakes on top to make a lush bouquet. Add ribbon and a note card if you like.

SWEET TALK

Express yourself on a heart cut from pound cake dipped in melted pastel-colored frosting. Our message to you: everything sounds sweeter when it's written on a cupcake.

18 vanilla cupcakes baked in white paper liners

3 frozen pound cakes (10.75 ounces each), thawed (Sara Lee)

3 cans (16 ounces each) vanilla frosting

Red, green, yellow, orange, and purple food coloring

Conversation heart candies for decorating the platter (Necco Sweethearts)

1. Cut the pound cakes in half horizontally and lay the halves flat. Using a 3-inch heart-shaped cookie cutter, cut out 3 hearts from each half. (Tip: reserve the scraps for a layered dessert.)

2. Spread the top of the cupcakes with some of the vanilla frosting. Place a pound cake heart on top of each cupcake, pressing down to secure. Place the cupcakes in the freezer for 15 minutes, or until slightly frozen.

3. Tint ½ cup of the vanilla frosting red with the food coloring. Spoon the red frosting into a ziplock bag, press out the excess air, seal, and set aside. Divide the remaining frosting among five small microwavable bowls. Tint each bowl a different pastel color of pink, green, yellow, orange, and lavender. Cover with plastic wrap and set aside.

4. Working with one color of frosting at a time, microwave the frosting, stopping to

stir frequently, until it has the texture of lightly whipped cream, about 10 seconds. Remove 1 cupcake at a time from the freezer. Holding the cupcake by its paper bottom, dip it into the frosting just to cover the pound cake heart. Allow the excess frosting to drip off back into the bowl (see page 15). Turn right side up and let stand. Repeat with each color and the remaining cupcakes. If the frosting becomes too thick, reheat for several seconds, stirring well. Remove any excess frosting from the base of the hearts if necessary.

5. Snip a very small (^{1}/$_{16}$-inch) corner from the bag with the red frosting. Pipe sayings on top of the hearts. Place on a serving platter. Sprinkle the conversation heart candies around the platter at the base of the cupcakes.

RUBBER DUCKY

Time to get your ducks in a row. These are perfect for a baby shower, a birthday party, or even a crazy Easter bash. Making that ducky shape is as simple as attaching a doughnut hole and a marshmallow to a cupcake. Dip in melted yellow frosting and add a fruit chew beak and M&M eyes, and this little yellow flotilla is ready to quack.

24 **vanilla cupcakes baked in yellow paper liners (see Sources)**

2 **cans (16 ounces each) plus 1 cup vanilla frosting**

Yellow food coloring

12 **marshmallows**

20 **plain doughnut holes**

14 **orange fruit chews (Tootsie Fruit Rolls, Starburst)**

48 **brown mini candy-coated chocolates (M&M's Minis)**

1. Tint 1 can plus $3/4$ cup of the vanilla frosting bright yellow with the yellow food coloring. Spoon the yellow frosting into a microwavable measuring cup; cover with plastic wrap. Spoon $1/4$ cup of the vanilla frosting into a ziplock bag, press out the excess air, seal, and set aside.

2. Cut the marshmallows in half on the diagonal with scissors. Spread some of the vanilla frosting from the remaining can on top of a cupcake. For the head, place a doughnut hole on one side. For the tail, arrange the cut marshmallow, pointed end up, on the edge on the opposite side (see the photo on page 14). Repeat to make 20 heads-up ducks. To make the bottoms-up ducks, place a cut marshmallow in the center of each of the remaining 4 cupcakes, pointed end up. Spread vanilla frosting up the sides of the doughnut holes and marshmallows on the cupcakes to fill in the gaps and smooth. Place the cupcakes in the freezer for 15 minutes, or until slightly frozen.

3. Microwave the yellow frosting, stopping to stir frequently, until it has the texture of lightly whipped cream, about 45 seconds. Remove 1 cupcake at a time from the freezer. Holding the cupcake by its paper bottom, dip it into the yellow frosting just up to the liner. Allow the excess frosting to drip off back into the cup (see page 15). Turn right side up and let stand. Repeat with the remaining cupcakes. If the frosting becomes too thick, reheat for several seconds, stirring well.

4. For the beaks, cut 10 of the orange fruit chews in half. Shape each piece into a $3/4$-by-$1^1/2$-inch oval. Fold the fruit chew almost in half, then pinch at the fold and shape to look like an open beak. Place the folded edge of the fruit chew on the front of the doughnut hole head, pressing gently to secure. For the feet, cut the remaining 4 fruit chews in half on the diagonal. Flatten each piece into a 1-by-$1^1/2$-by-$1^1/2$-inch triangle. Shape the short end to make the webbed feet. Score the top with a small knife. Insert the pointed end of the feet at the base of the tail on the bottoms-up cupcakes. Snip a small ($1/8$-inch) corner from the bag with the vanilla frosting. Pipe a white dot on either side of the head for the eyes and add the mini brown candies.

SHOWER HEADS

The mom-to-be will appreciate being showered with adorable little baby droplets of mini cupcakes streaming out of a delicious jumbo-size cupcake showerhead.

24 mini vanilla cupcakes baked in blue paper liners (see Sources)

1 jumbo vanilla cupcake baked in a silver foil liner (Reynolds)

1 can (16 ounces) plus 1 cup vanilla frosting

Black, red, orange, and yellow food coloring

1 cup canned chocolate frosting

1/2 cup each light and dark blue decorating sugars (see Sources)

24 vanilla wafers

Brown and pink candy-coated chocolate-covered sunflower seeds (Sunny Seed Drops)

Pink decors (Cake Mate)

1 teaspoon blue nonpareils (Cake Mate)

Blue paper

1. Tint 1/4 cup of the vanilla frosting gray with the black food coloring. Tint 1/4 cup of the vanilla frosting pink with the red food coloring. Tint 1/8 cup of the vanilla frosting orange with the orange food coloring and 1/8 cup yellow with the yellow food coloring. Tint 1/4 cup of the chocolate frosting black with the black food coloring. Spoon the tinted frostings into separate ziplock bags, press out the excess air, and seal. Spoon 1/3 cup of the vanilla frosting into each of three separate microwavable bowls. Tint one bowl a very pale pink with the red food coloring, one bowl a very pale beige with the red food coloring and a small amount of the chocolate frosting, and the last bowl light brown with some of the chocolate frosting. Cover each bowl with plastic wrap to prevent drying. Spoon the remaining chocolate frosting into a ziplock bag, press out the excess air, and seal.

2. Place the light and dark blue decorating sugars in separate shallow bowls. Spread the tops of the mini cupcakes with the remaining vanilla frosting and smooth. Roll the edges of 12 of the mini cupcakes in the light blue sugar and the remaining 12 in the dark blue sugar (see page 17). Transfer the cupcakes to a cookie sheet.

3. Heat one of the tinted bowls of frosting in the microwave for about 5 seconds, stirring well, and continue to microwave for several seconds more, until the frosting has the texture of lightly whipped cream. Working with 8 vanilla wafers at a time, place the round side of a cookie into the melted frosting to coat. Flip the cookie over onto a fork and allow the excess frosting to drip off back into the bowl. Transfer the cookie to the top of one of the mini frosted cupcakes, round side up. Continue the technique with the other two bowls of tinted frostings and the remaining 16 vanilla wafers.

4. Snip a very small ($1/16$-inch) corner from each of the bags with the tinted frosting, except the gray frosting. For the faces, pipe hair, eyes, and mouths with the frostings on the vanilla wafers, using the photo on page 133 as a guide. Add the candy-coated sunflower seeds for the noses and the pink decors for the cheeks.

5. Snip a $1/4$-inch corner from the bag with the gray frosting. For the showerhead, pipe a large dollop of frosting on top of the jumbo cupcake and spread to make smooth. Sprinkle the top with the blue nonpareils and pipe a decorative edge around the cupcake with the remaining gray frosting.

6. Set the jumbo cupcake on its side to look like a showerhead. Fan the mini cupcake heads out below. Cut out water-drop shapes from blue paper and place around the heads to complete the baby shower heads.

PLASTIC EASTER EGGS

The perfectly smooth eggshells—so pretty you won't want to open them, so tasty you'll want to eat them—are created by coating the inside of plastic eggs with colorful melted candy. After the candy hardens, pop them out and fill them with your favorite small candies.

12 **vanilla cupcakes baked in green paper liners (see Sources)**

³/₄ **cup each yellow, purple, and pink candy melting wafers (Wilton)**

2 **teaspoons vegetable oil**

1 **bag (12 ounces) spice drops**

¹/₂ **cup granulated sugar**

1 **can (16 ounces) vanilla frosting**

Green and yellow food coloring

2 **tablespoons flower-shaped decors (Cake Mate)**

³/₄ **cup small candies (Jelly Belly jelly beans and bunny corn)**

6 **plastic Easter eggs (3¹/₂ inches long; see Sources)**

1. Place each color of the candy melting wafers in a separate microwavable bowl. Working with one color at a time, microwave for 10 seconds, stir, and repeat until the candies are melted and smooth, about 1 minute.

2. Line a cookie sheet with wax paper and place in the refrigerator. Lightly oil a paper towel with the vegetable oil. Rub the inside of each plastic egg half with the oiled paper towel. Using your finger or a small brush, generously coat the inside of an oiled plastic egg half with one color of the melted candy. Transfer the egg, open side down, to the cookie sheet in the refrigerator. Repeat with the remaining melted candy and plastic eggs. After a few minutes, check and touch up any eggs where the candy is too thin or there is a hole. Return to the refrigerator until set, about 5 minutes.

3. Carefully remove the hardened candy from the plastic eggs without breaking it

(you will need 8 egg halves of each color, so make extra in case of breakage). Repeat with the other colored melted candy to get 24 egg halves (12 whole eggs).

4. Press 4 like-colored spice drops together and roll out on a work surface sprinkled with the granulated sugar to a $\frac{1}{8}$-inch thickness. Cut out small flower and leaf shapes using the templates on page 135 and $\frac{1}{2}$-by-4$\frac{1}{2}$-inch strips. Repeat with like-colored spice drops to make a total of 24 flowers, 24 leaves, and 12 strips.

5. Spoon $\frac{1}{2}$ cup of the vanilla frosting into a ziplock bag, press out the excess air, and seal. Tint the remaining vanilla frosting bright green with the green and yellow food coloring. Spoon the green frosting into two ziplock bags, press out the excess air, and seal. Snip a small ($\frac{1}{8}$-inch) corner from each bag. Pipe grass on top of the cupcakes using the squeeze-release-pull technique (see page 13). Add flower decors to the top of the cupcakes.

6. Snip a small ($\frac{1}{8}$-inch) corner from the bag with the vanilla frosting. Pipe a line around the open end of the eggs. Fill the eggs with the candies. Press the egg halves together to seal. Place the sealed eggs on top of the frosted cupcakes. Pipe more vanilla frosting along the seams and attach a spice drop strip as the band around each egg. Pipe a dot of vanilla frosting on top and add 2 flowers and 2 leaves to each. Pipe white dots of frosting to make centers for the candy flowers. Pipe extra grass around the eggs, if necessary.

MUM'S THE WORD

Moms love mums. We cut mini marshmallows on the diagonal and dipped the sticky side in colored sugar to make dozens of pink, yellow, purple, blue, and orange petals. Your mums will leave Mom speechless.

8 vanilla cupcakes baked in orange paper liners (see Sources)

1/4 cup each blue, white, light yellow, bright pink, bright yellow, orange, and purple decorating sugars (or see page 16 to tint your own)

1 bag (10.5 ounces) flavored mini marshmallows (assorted pastel colors)

1 bag (10.5 ounces) mini marshmallows

1 cup canned vanilla frosting

40 pastel-colored licorice pastels (Jelly Belly)

Green licorice twists (Twizzlers Rainbow Twists)

1. Place each colored sugar in a separate shallow bowl. Sort out 22 like-colored marshmallows for each cupcake. Make the petals for each cupcake by cutting the 22 mini marshmallows in half on the diagonal, allowing all of the marshmallow pieces to fall into one of the colored sugars. Shake the bowl and press the cut sides of the marshmallows into the sugar to coat. Repeat with the remaining marshmallows and colored sugars.

2. Spread a thin layer of frosting on top of 1 cupcake. Starting along the outside edge of the cupcake, arrange like-colored marshmallow petals, sugared sides up, close together. Continue with another 2 rows of the same color marshmallows to almost completely cover the cupcake. Repeat with the remaining frosting, cupcakes, and marshmallows.

3. For the stamens, insert 5 like-colored licorice pastels in the center of each cupcake. Arrange the flower cupcakes on a serving platter. Trim the green licorice twists to look like stems and place on the platter.

HEAD OF THE CLASS

Here's a bird's-eye view of the graduating class. Each cap made from Reese's Peanut Butter Cups and After Eight mints sits atop a unique head of hair—or lack of it—crafted from chewing gum, cereal, frosting, or sugar. Make liners, tassels, and buttons to match your school colors.

10 **vanilla cupcakes baked in liners to match school colors (Reynolds)**

1 **can (16 ounces) vanilla frosting**

Yellow, red, and blue food coloring

1 **cup canned chocolate frosting**

¹/₄ **teaspoon unsweetened cocoa powder (Hershey's)**

¹/₄ **cup each orange, red, and yellow cereal O's (Froot Loops)**

12 **sticks yellow gum (Juicy Fruit)**

3 **tablespoons chocolate sprinkles**

2 **teaspoons white decorating sugar (see Sources)**

12 **mini chocolate and peanut butter cups, unwrapped (Reese's)**

12 **chocolate-covered thin mint candies or graham crackers (After Eight or Afrika cookies)**

10 **blue mini candy-coated chocolates (M&M's Minis)**

1. Tint ¹/₄ cup of the vanilla frosting orange with the yellow and red food coloring. Tint 3 tablespoons of the vanilla frosting blue. Spoon each color frosting into a separate ziplock bag. Spoon the chocolate frosting into a ziplock bag, press out the excess air, and seal the bags. Tint the remaining vanilla frosting light tan with red food coloring and the cocoa powder. Cover with plastic wrap and set aside.

2. Frost the cupcakes with a mound of the light tan frosting and smooth. For the ears, press 2 orange cereal O's on opposite sides of each frosted cupcake, just above the paper liner. Add hair as directed on the next page.

FOR SHORT BLOND HAIR: Cut 6 gum sticks in half crosswise. Using pinking shears, cut one short end to create a zigzag end. Using straight scissors, cut long strips, leaving a $1/2$-inch section uncut at the straight end. Press the gum pieces into the frosting to create 2 layers of hair.

FOR LONG BLOND HAIR: Using scissors and 4 sticks of the yellow gum, cut lengthwise strips $1/8$ inch wide from one short end of each gum stick, leaving $1/2$ inch at the other short end uncut. Cut the remaining 2 sticks in half crosswise and cut more thin strips, leaving $1/2$ inch at the other short end uncut. Press the long pieces into the frosting at the sides and back of the cupcake and add the short pieces to the front to make bangs.

FOR CURLY HAIR: Starting at the bottom edge of a frosted cupcake, press the red cereal O's into the frosting in overlapping circles, leaving the top empty for the graduation cap. Repeat with the yellow cereal O's and another cupcake.

FOR FROSTING HAIR: Snip a small ($1/8$-inch) corner from the bags with each of the tinted frostings. To make the curls, pipe the orange frosting all over one cupcake. Repeat with the chocolate frosting and another cupcake. To make shaggy hair, start at the edge of the cupcake and, using the squeeze-release-pull technique (see page 13), pipe rows of hair with the chocolate frosting. To make parted hair, mark a line down the center of a cupcake with a toothpick and pipe rows of chocolate frosting from the center line on either side, leaving a small gap to show the tan frosting.

FOR A CREW CUT: Place the chocolate sprinkles in a small shallow bowl. Roll the frosted cupcake in the sprinkles to cover (see page 17).

FOR A BALD HEAD: Sprinkle the cupcake with the white decorating sugar to cover.

3. Press a chocolate peanut butter cup, large end down, on top of each cupcake, adding a dot of frosting to secure if necessary. Pipe a dot of chocolate frosting on top of each peanut butter cup and add the chocolate-covered mint or cookie as the mortarboard. For the tassel, starting from the center of the mortarboard, pipe several lines of blue frosting, allowing the frosting to overhang the edge of the chocolate. Press a blue candy on top. Arrange the cupcakes on a platter in 2 rows.

NINETEENTH HOLE

By the time you get done with the back nine, it's time to sit back and enjoy a cupcake at the nineteenth hole. Our links include a well-maintained fairway of close-cropped frosting grass, a green that is groomed to perfection with a coating of sugar, and a challenging sand trap filled with vanilla cookie crumbs.

24 vanilla cupcakes, 6 baked in white paper liners and 18 baked in green paper liners (see Sources)

¹/₂ cup ground vanilla wafers

2 cans (16 ounces each) vanilla frosting

Green food coloring

¹/₂ cup green decorating sugar (Cake Mate)

1 yellow flat candy (Smarties)

1 yellow licorice pastel (Jelly Belly)

1 tablespoon white nonpareils (see Sources)

4 white gum balls

1 teaspoon light corn syrup

1 2-inch piece strawberry fruit leather (Fruit by the Foot)

1 thin pretzel stick (Bachman)

1 large chocolate chip (Hershey's Mini Kisses)

1. Place the cookie crumbs in a shallow bowl. Spread the tops of the 6 cupcakes in white paper liners with vanilla frosting and smooth. Roll the tops in the crumbs to cover (see page 17). Spoon 2 tablespoons vanilla frosting into a small ziplock bag, press out the excess air, and seal. Tint the remaining frosting green with the food coloring.

2. Place the green decorating sugar in a small shallow bowl. Spread the tops of 7 of the remaining cupcakes with green frosting and smooth. Roll the tops in the

sugar to cover. Spread a thin layer of green frosting over the remaining 11 cupcakes. Spoon the remaining green frosting into two ziplock bags, press out the excess air, and seal.

3. Arrange the cupcakes on a serving platter, grouping the crumb-topped cupcakes and the sugar-topped cupcakes together (see the photo on the opposite page). Snip a small ($\frac{1}{8}$-inch) corner from the bags with the green frosting. Pipe grass over the green-frosted cupcakes and around the perimeter of the sugar-topped cupcakes using the squeeze-release-pull technique (see page 13).

4. For the tee, snip a small ($\frac{1}{8}$-inch) corner from the bag with the vanilla frosting and pipe a dot on one end of the yellow flat candy. Attach the licorice pastel and insert into 1 of the cupcakes at the tee position. Place the white nonpareils in a small shallow bowl. Roll the gum balls in the corn syrup to coat and then roll them in the nonpareils to coat. Place 1 ball on top of the tee and the others on other cupcakes.

5. For the flag, fold the fruit leather in half around one end of the pretzel stick. Using clean scissors, cut into a triangular flag shape. Pipe the number "19" on the flag with the vanilla frosting. Insert the pretzel stick in the center of the sugar-topped cupcake grouping. For the hole, add the large chocolate chip at the base of the pretzel, pointed end down.

SHUTTLECOCKS

If your opponent doesn't return the bird, check to see if he ate it. We've freshened up the game of badminton by turning the shuttlecocks into cupcakes. To keep service from going into overtime, the feathers can be made up to 1 week in advance.

12 **vanilla cupcakes baked in paper liners**

12 **mini vanilla cupcakes baked in paper liners**

2 **cups white candy melting wafers (Wilton)**

1 **can (16 ounces) vanilla frosting**

12 **round (2¹/₂-inch) flat butter cookies (LU)**

12 **large red gumdrops (Farley's)**

1. Make multiple copies of the feather template, place on cookie sheets, and cover with pieces of wax paper. Divide the white candy melting wafers between two ziplock bags; do not seal the bags. Working with one bag at a time, microwave for 10 seconds to soften. Massage the wafers in the bag, return to the microwave, and repeat the process until the candy is smooth, about 1¹/₂ minutes (see page 18). Press out the excess air and seal the bag.

2. Snip a small (¹/₈-inch) corner from each bag. Working on 1 feather at a time, outline the template on the wax paper. Tap the pan lightly to smooth the surface. Repeat to make 140 feathers using both bags of melted candy (you will need about 11 feathers per cupcake; allow a few extra for breakage). Refrigerate until set, about 5 minutes. (The feathers can be made up to 1 week in advance; keep in a cool, dry place.)

3. Trim the tops of all the cupcakes to make flat. Remove the paper liners from all the cupcakes. Spread a dot of vanilla frosting on one side of the butter cookies.

Place a standard cupcake on top of the frosted cookie, cut side down. Place another dot of frosting on top of the cupcake and add the mini cupcake, cut side down, to make the shuttlecock shape.

4. Working on 1 shuttlecock at a time, spread vanilla frosting over the double cupcake to cover. Gently peel the feathers from the wax paper. Arrange 10 or 11 feathers, overlapping slightly, around the frosted cupcake, with the quills at the narrow end. Place a red gumdrop, flat side down, on the narrow end to make the top. Continue with the remaining feathers and cupcakes.

SAND CASTLES

We dropped our ice cream cones in the sand . . . and they couldn't be more delicious. In fact our whole castle is made from ice cream cones and cupcakes that have been rolled in sugar and cookie crumbs. Get the drift?

2 jumbo vanilla cupcakes baked in white paper liners

8 vanilla cupcakes baked in white paper liners

4 mini vanilla cupcakes baked in white paper liners

6 pieces striped gum (Fruit Stripe)

$1/4$ cup white chocolate chips (Nestlé)

6 thin pretzel sticks (Bachman)

1 can (16 ounces) vanilla frosting

2 wafer ice cream cones

3 sugar ice cream cones

5 graham cracker sticks

2 cups ground vanilla wafers

1 cup coarse white decorating sugar (see Sources)

3 tablespoons light corn syrup

1 kids' wafer ice cream cone (Joy)

2 oat cereal O's (Cheerios)

1. For the pennants, cut the striped gum with scissors into 2- to 3-inch-long tri-angles; shape by hand into waves before they harden. Line a cookie sheet with wax paper. Place the white chocolate chips in a ziplock bag; do not seal. Microwave for 10 seconds to soften. Massage the chips in the bag, return to the microwave, and repeat the process until the chips are smooth, about 1 minute (see page 18). Press out the excess air and seal the bag. Snip a small ($1/8$-inch) corner from the bag. Pipe a line of white chocolate along the short edge of each pennant. Attach each pennant to a pretzel, pressing the chocolate edge onto

the top part of the pretzel, and place on the cookie sheet. Refrigerate until set, about 5 minutes.

2. Spoon ¼ cup of the vanilla frosting into a small ziplock bag, press out the excess air, and seal.

3. Using a serrated knife, cut a 1½-inch piece from the bases of the 2 wafer cones; discard the bases. Cut a 2-inch piece from one of the sugar cones to make the small turret. Halve the graham sticks crosswise.

4. Combine the cookie crumbs with the white decorating sugar in a shallow bowl. Microwave the corn syrup in a small microwavable bowl until bubbly, about 5 seconds. Brush the sides of a cone with the hot syrup to coat and roll the cone in the crumb mixture. Repeat with all of the cones. Reheat the melted white chocolate for a few seconds to soften. Trim the pretzel of 1 pennant assembly to a 1-inch length. Pipe a dot of white chocolate in the opening of a cereal O. Put the base of the trimmed pretzel into the opening. Pipe a dot of white chocolate on the bottom of the cereal O, attach it to the top of one of the untrimmed sugar cones, and refrigerate until set, about 5 minutes.

5. Frost the cupcakes with the vanilla frosting and smooth. Roll the tops of the frosted cupcakes in the crumb mixture to coat (see page 17).

6. Press the trimmed wafer cones, cut side down, into 2 of the frosted and crumbed standard cupcakes. Snip a small (⅛-inch) corner from the bag with the vanilla frosting. Pipe a line of frosting around the inside edge of the wafer cones. For the 2 large turrets, place the untrimmed sugar cones inside the wafer cones, pointed end up, using the frosting line to secure. For the small turret, pipe a line of vanilla frosting on the inside edge of the kids' cone and add the trimmed sugar cone, using the frosting to secure. Add a dot of frosting to the tip of the small turret and top with the remaining cereal O.

7. Stack the cupcakes to make the castle's turrets, using the photo on the opposite page as a guide. Trim the pretzels as necessary and insert into the tops of some of the cupcakes. Attach the trimmed graham sticks, cut side down, along the outer edge of 1 of the cupcakes, using vanilla frosting to secure.

8. Arrange the cupcakes on several cake stands or a serving platter. Sprinkle the remaining cookie crumbs around the cupcakes to look like sand.

The House That Boo Built

A big old haunted house that's chocolate to the core; beware the tasty vermin scratching at the door. Chilly ghosts that float on dark chocolate dirt, and roaches with caramel cooked up for dessert. These treats remind us it's that time of year when even the cupcakes give us reason to fear.

malted milk ball

chocolate sugar cones

Sunny Seed Drops

chocolate
chunks

chocolate sprinkles

RIP

candy pumpkins

chocolate sandwich cookies

THE HAUNTED HOUSE

Talk about curb appeal! Our haunted house is so pretty you won't want to eat it. But dive in, because almost every part is made from decadent dark chocolate: ice cream cones for the turrets, cookies for the shutters and door, candies for the finials and stones, and chocolate crumbs for the dirt.

2 **jumbo chocolate cupcakes baked in brown paper liners (see Sources)**

5 **chocolate cupcakes baked in brown paper liners (see Sources)**

2 **chocolate cupcakes baked in orange paper liners (see Sources)**

1 **cup dark cocoa candy melting wafers (Wilton)**

1 **tablespoon orange sprinkles (Cake Mate)**

2 **chocolate ice cream cones (Oreo)**

2 **round chocolate candies (chocolate-covered peanuts or malted milk balls)**

3 **oblong chocolate sandwich cookies (or cut oblong shape from flat chocolate cookies)**

1 **tube (4.25 ounces) white decorating icing (Cake Mate)**

3 **chocolate chews (Tootsie Rolls)**

1 **can (16 ounces) dark chocolate frosting**

¹/₄ **cup chocolate chunks (Saco Foods)**

1 **cup chocolate sprinkles**

4 **yellow candy-coated chocolate-covered sunflower seeds or chocolates (Sunny Seed Drops, M&M's Minis)**

¹/₂ **cup ground chocolate cookies (optional; Oreos, Famous Chocolate Wafers)**

Candy pumpkins (optional)

1. Place the tree template (page 156) on a cookie sheet and cover with wax paper. Place the dark cocoa melting wafers in a ziplock bag; do not seal the bag. Microwave for about 10 seconds to soften. Massage the mixture and return to the microwave. Repeat the process until the candy is smooth, about 1 minute total (see page 18). Press out the excess air and seal the bag.

2. Snip a small ($\frac{1}{8}$-inch) corner from the bag with the melted candy and follow the template to pipe a tree. Sprinkle the branches with the orange sprinkles while the candy is still wet (see page 18). Transfer the cookie sheet to the refrigerator for 5 minutes, or until firm. Repeat to make 6 trees. Pipe a dot of melted candy on the tip of each ice cream cone and add a round chocolate candy. Refrigerate until the melted candy is set, about 5 minutes.

3. Gently twist 2 of the chocolate sandwich cookies apart, using a paring knife to remove the filling. Use a serrated knife to cut each piece in half lengthwise. For the shutters and door, trim each halved piece to $1\frac{1}{2}$ inches in length. For the tombstone, pipe "RIP" with the white decorating icing on the remaining whole cookie. For the windows, roll the chocolate chews into rectangles and cut each into a $\frac{3}{4}$-by-$1\frac{1}{4}$-inch piece.

4. Spoon $\frac{1}{4}$ cup of the chocolate frosting into a ziplock bag, press out the excess air, seal, and set aside. Spread the top of 1 jumbo cupcake with some of the remaining chocolate frosting and smooth. Arrange the chocolate chunks all around the outer edge of the cupcake. Place the chocolate sprinkles in a small shallow bowl. Spread the tops of the remaining cupcakes with the remaining chocolate frosting and smooth. Roll the edges of the cupcakes in the chocolate sprinkles (see page 17).

5. For the tower, place the chocolate chunk–edged jumbo cupcake on top of the other jumbo cupcake. Place a standard cupcake in a brown paper liner on top of that in the center of the chocolate chunks. Add an ice cream cone, open end down, to make the turret. Place the tower on a cake stand or serving platter. Snip a small ($\frac{1}{8}$-inch) corner from the bag with the chocolate frosting. Pipe dots of chocolate frosting on the sides of the top and middle cupcakes and attach the chocolate chew rectangles as the windows (1 on the top; 2 on the middle). Pipe chocolate lines to make the panes and add the cookie shutters on either side. For the door, add a set of trimmed cookie halves at the base of the tower.

Place a cupcake in an orange liner on either side of the tower. Stack the 4 remaining cupcakes to make 2 smaller towers behind the central one.

6. Place the remaining chocolate cone on top of one of the shorter towers, open end down, to make a turret. Gently peel the chocolate trees from the wax paper and insert randomly on top of the back and side cupcakes (you can trim the bases to make shorter trees if necessary). Add 2 yellow candies side by side on the top and lower cupcakes of the central tower and pipe chocolate dots as the eyes. Sprinkle the chocolate cookie crumbs around the base of the structure as dirt, if using. Add the cookie tombstone and the candy pumpkins, if using.

CHILLY GHOSTS

ez CUPCAKE

Did you just feel a chill go through the house? Someone must have opened the freezer and let out the ghosts. Each chilly ghost cupcake has an ice cream center, and the ghosts are whipped topping piped from a ziplock bag. Ghosts keep well in the freezer until just before haunting time.

24 **chocolate cupcakes baked in brown paper liners (see Sources)**

1¹/₂ **cups ground chocolate cookies (Oreos, Famous Chocolate Wafers, chocolate graham crackers)**

1 **can (16 ounces) chocolate frosting**

2 **containers (8 ounces each) frozen whipped topping (Cool Whip), thawed in refrigerator**

24 **1¹/₂-inch balls of your favorite flavor ice cream**

48 **multicolored candy-coated chocolate-covered sunflower seeds or chocolates (Sunny Seed Drops, M&M's Minis)**

1. Using a paring knife, cut out a cone-shaped piece 1¹/₂ inches in diameter from the center of each cupcake and reserve for the top of the cupcake (see the photo on page 159).

2. Place the chocolate cookie crumbs in a small shallow bowl. Spread the chocolate frosting around the top of the cupcakes, leaving the opening unfrosted. Roll the tops in the cookie crumbs to cover (see page 17).

3. Divide the whipped topping between two ziplock bags. Snip a ³/₄-inch corner from each bag. Place the ice cream balls in the cupcake openings, pressing the ice cream down into the holes. Place the cone-shaped piece of cake on top, flat side down, and press down slightly (see the photo on page 159). Pipe a circle of the whipped topping around the base of the cone cake. Pipe a smaller circle on top of the ice cream and the whipped topping to cover the cake, then pipe a third layer of whipped topping, using a squeeze-release-pull motion (see page 13), to make the peaked ghost head.

4. Insert 2 matching candies for the eyes, pointed ends into the whipped topping. Serve immediately, or place in the freezer until ready to serve (if frozen, let the cupcakes stand at room temperature for 10 minutes before serving).

INDIAN CORN

Amaize your crowd with this crafty centerpiece inspired by the dried harvest corn decorations that grace doorways each fall. The kernels are gourmet jelly beans in beautiful autumn shades. Sheets of toasted phyllo dough form the tawny corn husks.

24 vanilla cupcakes baked in white paper liners

3 sheets phyllo dough, thawed

Vegetable cooking spray

1 can (16 ounces) vanilla frosting

¼ teaspoon unsweetened cocoa powder (Hershey's)

About 4 cups assorted small gourmet jelly beans in russet, orange, gold, cream, and brown (Jelly Belly)

1. Preheat the oven to 350°F. Line a cookie sheet with crumpled foil. Cut the phyllo sheets crosswise into 3-inch-wide strips, tapering both ends. Drape the stacked husks on the prepared pan, shaping them over the crumpled foil to make curves. Spray lightly with vegetable cooking spray. Bake until the phyllo is golden brown, 4 to 5 minutes. Transfer to a wire rack and allow to cool completely. (The husks can be made up to 1 day in advance and kept in an airtight container.)

2. Tint the vanilla frosting pale beige with the cocoa powder.

3. Working with 3 cupcakes at a time, spread some of the pale beige frosting on top. Arrange about 5 straight rows of jelly beans, side by side and close together, on each cupcake. (Try to select flavors that go well together, such as toasted marshmallow, banana, cappuccino, and chocolate pudding.) Repeat with the remaining cupcakes, frosting, and jelly beans.

4. For each ear of corn, place 3 cupcakes end to end on a serving platter, aligning the rows of jelly beans. Arrange the phyllo husks on either side of the corn.

PANTRY PETS

Scared to open the pantry door? Better arm yourself with a fork. The yummy combo of a date body, caramel wings, and chocolate heads will make you want to stock roaches in your kitchen all the time.

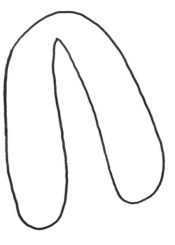

24 mini chocolate cupcakes baked in brown paper liners (see Sources)

1¹/₂ cups canned chocolate frosting

24 soft caramels (Kraft)

12 brown candy-coated chocolates (M&M's)

24 dates, pitted

1 cup cornflakes or rice flake cereal

1. Spoon ¹/₂ cup of the chocolate frosting into a ziplock bag, press out the excess air, seal, and set aside.

2. Spread the remaining chocolate frosting on top of the cupcakes and smooth.

3. Soften several caramels at a time in the microwave for 2 to 3 seconds. Roll out each piece on a sheet of wax paper to a ¹/₈-inch thickness. Cut out the cockroach wings using the template above and a pair of scissors (adjust the wing length according to the size of the dates). Score several lines on each wing with the back of a paring knife (see page 164). Repeat with the remaining caramels to make 24 pairs of wings.

4. For the heads, cut the brown candies in half with a paring knife.

5. Snip a very small (¹/₁₆-inch) corner from the bag with the frosting. For each roach, pipe a small dot of frosting on one short end of the date. Place the caramel wings to run lengthwise along the sides of the date, scored side up, and secure to the dot of frosting. For the head, pipe a dot of frosting on top of the caramel and add a brown candy piece, cut side against the caramel. Place the date on

top of a cupcake, and press a few cereal flakes into the frosting on each side. Pipe 2 wavy antennae, starting at the head and curving back over the wings. When all of the cupcakes have been assembled to this point, snip a larger ($\frac{1}{8}$-inch) corner from the bag and pipe 3 legs on each side of the cockroaches along the bottom edge of the caramel using the squeeze-release-pull technique (see page 13).

OH, RATS!

Uh-oh, uninvited guests are raiding the cheese platter. If the little rodent frosting teeth don't give you the heebie-jeebies, the fruit leather mouth and icky fruit chew tail certainly will. These two-cupcake rats wear a coating of PETA-approved chocolate sprinkles for fur.

RATS

6 vanilla cupcakes baked in brown paper liners (see Sources)

6 mini vanilla cupcakes baked in brown paper liners (see Sources)

30 pink fruit chews (Jolly Rancher, Starburst, Laffy Taffy, Tootsie Fruit Rolls)

$1/4$ cup canned vanilla frosting

1 can (16 ounces) dark chocolate frosting

6 marshmallows

1 roll (0.75 ounce) strawberry fruit leather (Fruit by the Foot)

1 cup chocolate sprinkles

12 red and 6 brown mini candy-coated chocolates (M&M's Minis)

1. Soften 3 pink fruit chews at a time in the microwave for 2 to 3 seconds. For the tail, press the 3 pieces together and roll between your hands to make a tapered rope about 5 inches long. Score the side of the candy rope with the back of a paring knife. Repeat to make 6 rat tails. Roll out the remaining 12 fruit chews on a piece of wax paper to a $1/8$-inch thickness. For the ears, cut out twelve $3/4$-inch ovals and pinch the smaller end to shape them. For the feet, cut the remaining fruit chews into twenty-four $3/4$-by-$1 1/2$-by-$1 1/2$-inch triangles. Cut notches in the short side to make the claws. Reheat and reroll the scraps as necessary to make all of the ears and feet.

2. Spoon the vanilla frosting and $1/4$ cup of the chocolate frosting into separate zip-lock bags, press out the excess air, and seal.

3. For the rats' muzzles, cut a 1-inch V-shaped notch from a short end of each marshmallow (see the photo below). Cut 2-inch-long ovals from the red fruit leather to fit the notched mouth openings and press into the notches of the muzzle to stick. Trim off any excess fruit leather with clean scissors. Trim a 1/2-inch slice from the opposite short end of the marshmallow to shorten the snout.

4. Place the chocolate sprinkles in a small shallow bowl. Spread a slight mound of chocolate frosting on top of the 6 standard cupcakes. Roll the tops of the frosted cupcakes in the sprinkles to coat (see page 17). Spread a thin layer of chocolate frosting over the top of the 6 mini cupcakes. Place a marshmallow muzzle, on a slight angle, close to one edge of each mini cupcake. Spread a thin layer of chocolate frosting up the sides of the marshmallow to cover. Carefully roll each mini cupcake and marshmallow in the sprinkles to coat. Remove any extra sprinkles that attach to the red fruit leather.

5. Insert the fruit chew ears on each side of the top edge of the mini cupcakes. Snip a small (1/8-inch) corner from the bags with the vanilla and chocolate frostings. Pipe 2 teeth on the top and 2 on the bottom of the open mouth with the vanilla frosting using the squeeze-release-pull technique (see page 13). Add 2 red candies as the eyes and 1 brown candy as the nose.

6. Assemble the mini and standard cupcakes to make the rats. For the standing rat, use a dot of chocolate frosting to secure the mini cupcake head on top of the standard cupcake. For the crouching rat, place the head cupcake next to the body cupcake. Arrange the tail and feet around each cupcake.

CHEESE AND CRACKERS

6 vanilla cupcakes baked in white paper liners

18 yellow fruit chews (Starburst, Laffy Taffy, Tootsie Fruit Rolls)

1 cup canned vanilla frosting

Yellow food coloring

Wheat crackers for garnish (optional)

1. For the cheese, soften 3 fruit chews at a time in the microwave for 2 to 3 seconds. Press the 3 fruit chews together and roll out on a sheet of wax paper to a 1/8-inch thickness. Cut out a 2-by-3-by-3-inch triangle. Use an apple corer, pastry tip, round cookie cutter, or lid from a small bottle to cut holes in the cheese. Repeat to make 6 cheese slices.

2. Tint the vanilla frosting yellow with the food coloring. Spread the top of the cupcakes with the yellow frosting and smooth. Place a slice of fruit chew cheese on top of each cupcake. Garnish the serving platter with the wheat crackers, if desired.

MR. BONES JANGLE

We take the skeleton out of the closet and put it on the cupcakes. Mr. Jangle's white chocolate bones are easy to make ahead of time. On All Hallow's Eve, just frost the cupcakes and add the bones!

11 **chocolate cupcakes baked in black paper liners (see Sources)**

12 **orange paper liners (see Sources)**

1 **black paper liner (see Sources)**

1 **cup white candy melting wafers (Wilton)**

1¹/₄ **cups ground chocolate cookies (Oreos, Famous Chocolate Wafers)**

1 **cup canned chocolate frosting**

Orange and black gummy worms or crunchy worms for garnish

1. Place the bone templates (page 171) on two cookie sheets. Cover with wax paper. Place the white candy melting wafers in a ziplock bag; do not seal the bag. Microwave for about 10 seconds to soften. Massage the mixture and return to the microwave. Repeat the process until the candy is smooth, about 1 minute (see page 18). Press out the excess air and seal.

2. Snip a small (¹/₈-inch) corner from the bag and, following the bone templates, pipe an outline. Fill in the bones with melted candy. Use a toothpick to pull the melted candy into the smaller areas. Tap the pans lightly to smooth the surface. Transfer the cookie sheets to the refrigerator for 5 minutes, or until firm.

3. Spoon the cookie crumbs into a small shallow bowl. Spread the frosting on top of the cupcakes and smooth. Roll the top of the cupcakes in the crumbs to cover completely (see page 17).

4. Place each cupcake in an orange paper liner. Arrange the cupcakes in a skeleton shape on a serving platter (see the photo on page 170). Carefully peel the bones from the wax paper and place them on the cupcakes as shown, pressing them into the crumbs and frosting. Garnish with gummy worms in paper liners.

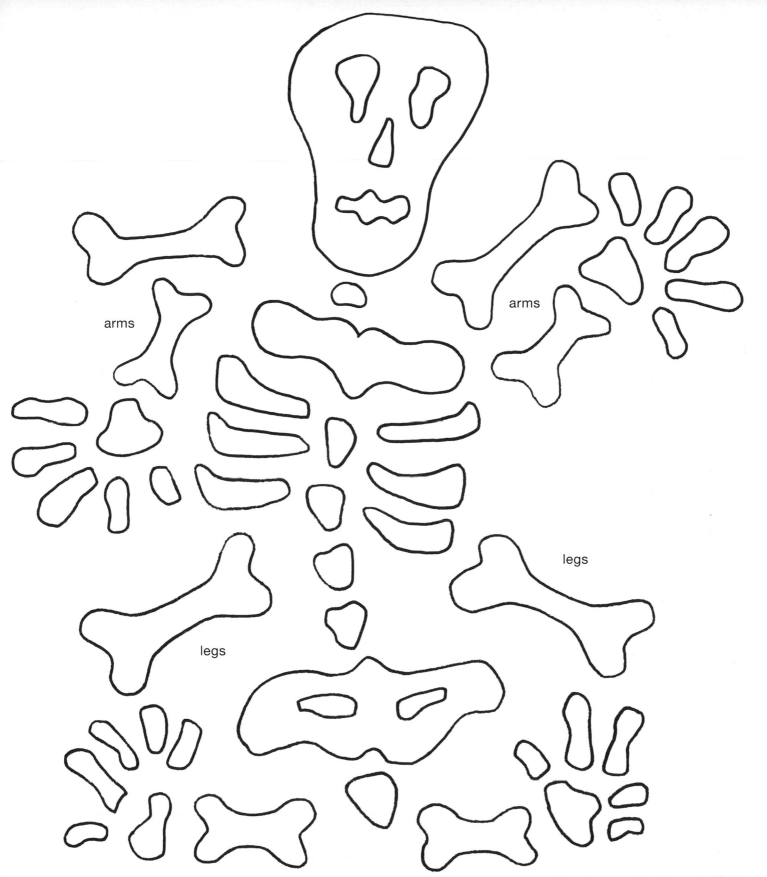

arms

arms

legs

legs

JACK-O'-LANTERNS

CUPCAKE

Who put the faux in the pumpkin glow? Yellow fruit chews, slightly smaller than the Tootsie Rolls underneath, let the light shine through. The pumpkins' ribs are piped from a ziplock bag, and the stems and split-rail fencing are crafted from pretzels.

6 jumbo Pumpkin-Spice Cupcakes (page 222) baked in orange paper liners (see Sources)

1 can (16 ounces) vanilla frosting

Orange food coloring

1/2 teaspoon unsweetened cocoa powder (Hershey's)

16 chocolate chews (Tootsie Rolls)

16 yellow fruit chews (Tootsie Fruit Rolls, Starburst, Laffy Taffy)

3 wheat twist pretzels (Rold Gold)

1. Tint the vanilla frosting deep orange with the orange food coloring and cocoa powder. Divide the frosting between two ziplock bags, press out the excess air, and seal.

2. Soften several chocolate chews at a time in the microwave for 2 to 3 seconds. Roll out each chew on a piece of wax paper to a 1/8-inch thickness. Using the outer line of the templates (page 174), cut out shapes using a small paring knife or scissors. Reheat and reroll the scraps as necessary to make all of the templates. Repeat with the yellow fruit chews and the inner line of the templates.

3. Place the yellow pieces on top of the chocolate pieces to make the eyes, mouths, and noses; set aside on wax paper.

4. Snip a 1/4-inch corner from the bags with the orange frosting. Starting at the top of a cupcake, pipe a thick line of frosting down the center. To make the pumpkin's ribs, pipe vertical lines on either side of the center line, tapering them slightly at the top and bottom. Repeat with the remaining cupcakes.

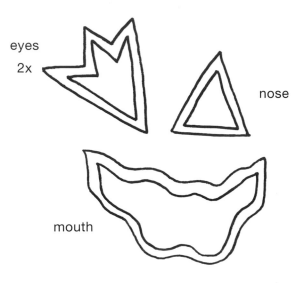

eyes
2x

nose

mouth

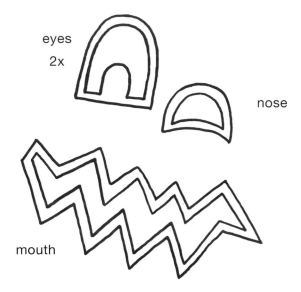

eyes
2x

nose

mouth

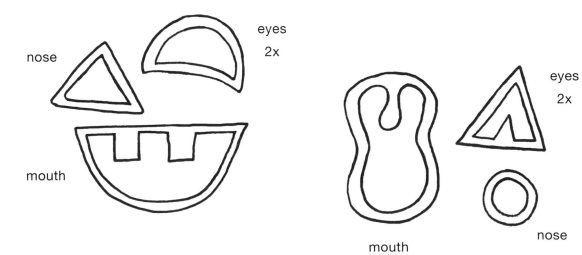

nose

eyes
2x

mouth

mouth

eyes
2x

nose

5. Arrange the face parts on top of the cupcakes (see the photo on page 173). For the stems, cut the wheat twist pretzels in half crosswise with a serrated knife and insert the cut ends into the top of the cupcakes. Arrange a few pretzel fences around the cupcakes on a serving platter (see directions below).

PRETZEL FENCES

$1/4$ cup white chocolate chips (Nestlé)

40 thin pretzel sticks (Rold Gold)

1. Line a cookie sheet with wax paper. Place the white chocolate chips in a ziplock bag; do not seal the bag. Microwave for about 10 seconds to soften. Massage the mixture and return to the microwave. Repeat the process until the chocolate is smooth, about 30 seconds total (see page 18). Press out the excess air and seal the bag.

2. Snip a small ($1/8$-inch) corner from the bag with the melted white chocolate. Place 2 thin pretzel sticks on the prepared cookie sheet about 2 inches apart. Pipe 2 dots of the melted white chocolate, at $3/4$-inch and $1 1/2$-inch intervals. Place 2 pretzel sticks crosswise, attaching at the chocolate dots to make a fence (see page 19). Repeat with the remaining pretzel sticks and white chocolate. Refrigerate until set, about 5 minutes.

IF I ONLY HAD A BRAIN

Our friend Straw Jack is more than just a stuffed shirt. His sack head has a caramel for the ruffle, and his pants sport a fruit chew waistband. He is held together with yellow and red taffy ropes and covered with spice drop patches. That Oreo crow is busy pulling shredded cereal from under Jack's graham cracker hat. Did we forget the brain?

13 **Pumpkin-Spice (page 222) or vanilla cupcakes baked in white paper liners**

1 **graham cracker**

3 **plain bread sticks**

2 **yellow, 2 blue, and 3 red fruit chews (Laffy Taffy, Starburst, Jolly Rancher)**

2 **soft caramels (Kraft)**

1 **each green, yellow, and orange spice drops**

1 **chocolate creme-filled sandwich cookie (Oreo)**

1/4 **cup canned dark chocolate frosting**

Black, yellow, orange, brown, and blue food coloring

1 **can (16 ounces) plus 1 cup vanilla frosting**

1 **shredded wheat biscuit (Post Original Shredded Wheat)**

1 **mini chocolate-coated mint (Junior Mints)**

3 **brown and 2 red candy-coated chocolates (M&M's)**

1. For the hat, using a serrated knife, cut a 2½-by-5-by-5-inch triangle from the graham cracker and remove the top 2 inches to give it a flat top. From the trimmed pieces, cut a ¼-by-4-inch strip for the brim. Cut 2 of the bread sticks with a serrated knife to make a 4-inch, a 2-inch, and a 1-inch piece. Leave the remaining bread stick whole.

2. Soften the 2 yellow and 2 blue fruit chews in the microwave for 2 to 3 seconds. Press the like-colored fruit chews together and roll out on a clean work surface to a 1/8-inch thickness, making a rectangle 1 1/2 by 4 inches. Using scissors or a pizza wheel, cut the yellow fruit-chew rectangle lengthwise into six 1/4-inch-wide strips. Twist 2 strips together; repeat two more times to make the 3 yellow ropes for the pants. Cut the blue fruit-chew rectangle lengthwise into 2 strips. Soften 2 of the red fruit chews in the microwave for 2 to 3 seconds. Press the fruit chews together and roll out on a clean work surface to a 1/8-inch thickness, making a rectangle 1 by 3 inches. Cut the red fruit-chew rectangle lengthwise into four 1/4-inch-wide strips. Twist 2 strips together; repeat to make the 2 red rope drawstrings for the shirt cuffs. Soften the remaining red fruit chew in the microwave for 2 to 3 seconds. Roll the fruit chew to a 1/8-inch thickness and cut into a 1/2-inch triangle for the nose.

3. For the neck ruffle, press the caramels together and roll out to a 1 1/2-by-3-inch rectangle. Trim the edges with a pair of scissors. For the patches on the pants, press the green and yellow spice drops on a clean work surface to flatten. Cut each piece into a 1/2-inch square.

4. Separate the sandwich cookie and scrape off the filling. For the crow's body, cut one cookie half in half with a serrated knife. For the crow's wings, cut the other cookie half into two 1/2-inch-wide pieces. For the beak, cut the orange spice drop in half lengthwise and cut a notch from one short end.

5. Tint the chocolate frosting black with the black food coloring. Tint 2 tablespoons of the vanilla frosting pale yellow with the food coloring. Spoon each color into a separate ziplock bag, press out the excess air, and seal. Tint 1 cup of the vanilla frosting orange with the orange food coloring. Spoon 2 tablespoons of the orange frosting into a small ziplock bag, press out the excess air, and seal. Tint 1/4 cup of the vanilla frosting light brown with the brown food coloring. Reserve 1/3 cup vanilla frosting. Tint the remaining frosting blue with the food coloring.

6. Spread 2 of the cupcakes with the reserved vanilla frosting and smooth. When frosting the remaining cupcakes, always spread in one direction to create soft ridges. Spread 1 cupcake with the light brown frosting. Spread 5 cupcakes with the orange frosting. Spread 4 cupcakes with the blue frosting. Spread the remaining cupcake with half orange and half blue frosting.

7. Assemble the cupcakes to create the scarecrow on a serving platter (see the photo on page 177). Add the bread stick pieces between the legs and under each arm to make the scarecrow's perch. For the stuffing, break apart the shredded wheat biscuit and add small pieces coming out of the end of the pants and sleeves and a few bits out of the hat and the splits in the shirt. Add the graham cracker hat and brim. Add the candy patches on the pants. Pinch the 2 blue rolled candy strips to create folds and place at the waist of the pants. Pinch the flattened caramel to create folds and place as the cinched neck ruffle. Arrange the yellow candy rope on the pants and the red drawstrings on the sleeves, trimming if necessary.

8. Add the chocolate cookie pieces to make the crow. Snip a small (1/8-inch) corner from the bags with the black, yellow, and orange frostings. Pipe a dot of black frosting and attach the chocolate-coated mint as the crow's head. Add the orange candy as the beak. Pipe a dot of yellow frosting as the eye.

9. Pipe a dot of black frosting and attach 1 brown candy to the scarecrow's hat. Pipe petals (see page 13) around the brown candy with the yellow frosting to make the sunflower. Add the remaining 2 brown candies for the eyes. Pipe a dot of yellow frosting on the brown candies as the highlight. Add the red fruit chew triangle as the nose. Pipe a dotted line with the black frosting for the mouth. Pipe black lines around the patches to look like stitching. Pipe 2 lines of orange frosting down the front of the shirt. Add the 2 red candies to make the buttons.

BLACK CATS

If a black cat crosses your path, it's your lucky day, especially if it's made from chocolate and coated in black sugar. The harvest moons underneath our kitties are cupcakes dipped in yellow frosting.

12 vanilla cupcakes baked in black paper liners (see Sources)

 1 cup dark cocoa candy melting wafers (Wilton)

 1 cup black decorating sugar (see Sources)

 1 cup plus 2 tablespoons canned vanilla frosting
    Yellow food coloring

1. Place a cat template (page 182) on a cookie sheet and cover with wax paper.

2. Place the cocoa candy melting wafers in a ziplock bag; do not seal the bag. Microwave for 10 seconds to soften. Massage and return to the microwave. Repeat the process until the candy is smooth, about 45 seconds total (see page 18). Press out the excess air and seal.

3. Snip a small (¹/₈-inch) corner from the bag and pipe the outline of the cat on the wax paper. Fill in the cat with the melted candy. Tap the pan lightly to smooth the surface. Sprinkle the top of the wet melted candy with the black sugar to cover. Repeat to make 13 cats (the extra one is in case of breakage). Refrigerate until set, about 5 minutes.

4. Tint the vanilla frosting bright yellow with the food coloring. Spoon 2 tablespoons of the yellow frosting into a small ziplock bag, press out the excess air, and seal.

5. Spoon the remaining yellow frosting into a shallow microwavable bowl. Heat the frosting in the microwave, stopping to stir frequently, until it has the texture of lightly whipped cream, 10 to 15 seconds.

6. Holding a cupcake by its paper liner, dip it into the frosting just up to the edge of the liner. Allow the excess frosting to drip off back into the bowl (see page 15). Carefully invert the cupcake and place on a cookie sheet. Repeat with the remaining cupcakes. If the frosting becomes too thick, microwave for several seconds, stirring well.

7. Snip a very small ($\frac{1}{16}$-inch) corner from the bag with the yellow frosting and pipe the slanted eyes on the cats. Snip a larger corner from the bag and pipe a dot of yellow frosting near one edge of each cupcake. Carefully peel the cats from the wax paper and place one on top of each cupcake, using the dot of frosting to secure.

STUFFED TURKEYS

Turkey and stuffing with the fixings and dessert, all in one. Now that's efficient! No problem getting a golden skin on this bird: just roll out a caramel and stretch it tight over the frosting.

12 **vanilla cupcakes baked in orange paper liners (see Sources)**

1 **can (16 ounces) plus $^1/_2$ cup vanilla frosting**

Green and yellow food coloring

1 **cup cornflakes or rice flake cereal**

72 **soft caramels (Kraft), unwrapped**

12 **wheat sticks (Pringles)**

$^1/_2$ **cup wheat and barley cereal (Grape-Nuts or crushed cornflakes)**

2 **tablespoons green nonpareils (Cake Mate)**

1. Spoon $^1/_4$ cup of the vanilla frosting into a ziplock bag, press out the excess air, and seal. Tint $^1/_4$ cup of the vanilla frosting light green with the green and yellow food coloring.

2. Place the corn or rice cereal in a medium bowl. Heat the green frosting in a small microwavable bowl, stopping to stir frequently, until it has the texture of lightly whipped cream, 10 to 15 seconds. Pour the heated frosting over the cereal, tossing to coat well. Spread the cereal on a cookie sheet lined with wax paper to dry.

3. Soften 4 caramels at a time in the microwave for 3 to 4 seconds. Press the caramels together and roll out on a clean work surface into a 3$^1/_2$-inch circle. Using scissors and following the template above, cut a turkey skin from the caramel. Repeat to make 12 skins. Place the turkey skins on a sheet of wax paper. Cut the wheat sticks into 2-inch lengths. Soften a caramel in the microwave for 3 to 4 seconds. For the drumstick, press the caramel around 1 inch of a wheat stick

and form it into a drumstick shape. Repeat with the remaining caramels and wheat sticks to make 24 drumsticks.

4. Spread the tops of the cupcakes with a mound of vanilla frosting. Place a caramel turkey skin on top of each cupcake. Tuck the edge of the caramel in $1/4$ inch from the edge of the cupcake, using a small spatula or a butter knife to push the caramel into the frosting, making the turkey body look plumper. Pinch the ends of the caramel at the opening; some of the frosting will come out of the opening. Press the wheat and barley cereal into the frosting at the opening to look like the stuffing. Sprinkle the cereal with the green nonpareils for parsley.

5. Lightly brush the caramel on each side of the cereal stuffing with a drop of water. Attach a caramel drumstick to each side of the opening (see photo on the opposite page for placement). Repeat for remaining cupcakes and drumsticks.

6. Snip a small ($1/8$-inch) corner from the bag with the vanilla frosting. Pipe a few dots of frosting at the end of each wheat stick to look like the end of the leg bone. Add the green cereal as lettuce around the edge of each cupcake, using dots of frosting to secure if necessary.

Hooray for Holly Days

These are zany, festive holly days, where blow-up Santas are a cupcake craze, blue poinsettias are all the rage, and punch makes elves behave in wacky ways. Where a walrus and a polar bear can share a doughnut without a care, and a gingerbread cupcake village makes tasty fare. Where cupcake trees are festooned with stars you can see through, and a Rudolph cupcake says, "Happy holidays to you."

decorating sugar

hard candy

sugar cookie dough

EYE-CANDY ORNAMENTS

As colorful as stained glass on a cupcake, these ornaments are created from store-bought cookie dough baked with crushed hard candies in the center. They are so pretty that you may want to bake extra for your tree.

12 vanilla cupcakes baked in silver foil liners (Reynolds)

1 recipe dough from Quick Sugar Cookies (page 225)

12 thin pretzel sticks (Bachman)

3/4 cup each red, green, and blue crushed hard candies (Jolly Rancher)

1/3 cup each blue, green, red, and yellow decorating sugars (Cake Mate)

1/3 cup light corn syrup

1 can (16 ounces) vanilla frosting

Yellow food coloring

3/4 cup coarse white decorating sugar (see Sources)

1. Preheat the oven to 350°F and line two cookie sheets with parchment paper. Using the template (opposite page) or a homemade cookie cutter made from the template, cut the rolled-out cookie dough into 12 ornament shapes following the directions on page 20. Transfer the cutouts to the prepared pans, spacing about 1 inch apart. Cut out the centers of the ornaments with a small paring knife, lid, or round cookie cutter, removing a 1½-inch circle from each. Use a straw to make a small hole at the top of the ornament. Press a pretzel stick into the cookie dough at the base of the cookie cutouts to form the support for the ornament (see page 19); the placement of the pretzels should be varied to give the finished ornaments a tumbled look.

2. Bake the cookies until just golden and firm to the touch, 7 to 10 minutes. Transfer the pans to wire racks. Spoon about 2 tablespoons of the crushed candies (keeping the colors separate) in the center of each cookie cutout. Return the pans to the oven and bake until the candies are just melted and smooth on top, about 2 minutes (see page 21). Transfer the pans to the wire racks and allow to cool completely.

3. Carefully peel the candy-filled cookies from the parchment paper. Place the blue, green, and red decorating sugars in separate shallow bowls. Heat the corn syrup in the microwave until bubbly, 8 to 10 seconds. Working on 1 cookie at a time and using a small brush, lightly paint corn syrup on the smooth side of the circular cookie surface. Dip the cookie into the matching colored sugar to coat. Brush off the excess sugar from the candy area with a dry brush. Repeat with the remaining cookies and sugars.

4. Tint 1/2 cup of the vanilla frosting yellow with the food coloring. Spoon the yellow frosting into a ziplock bag, press out the excess air, and seal. Snip a small (1/8-inch) corner from the bag and pipe decorative lines at the top of the ornament to make the hanger. Sprinkle the frosted area with the yellow decorating sugar.

5. Place the coarse white decorating sugar in a small shallow bowl. Frost the tops of the cupcakes with the remaining vanilla frosting and swirl. Roll the edge of the frosted cupcakes in the sugar (see page 17). Arrange the cupcakes on a serving platter. Just before serving, insert the ornaments' pretzel sticks into the tops of the cupcakes.

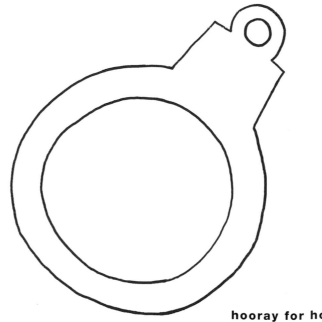

PUNCH-DRUNK ELVES

Goofy, Loopy, Droopy, Sloppy, and Punch. How'd they get so drunk? We spiked the cake with rum flavor. Their hats are custom-cut cookies; pretzels on the back hold them in place. The taffy ears and jelly bean noses flush pink from all that booze.

12 **Spice-Rum Cupcakes (page 221) baked in green paper liners (see Sources)**

1 **recipe dough from Quick Sugar Cookies (page 225) or 12 whole rectangular graham crackers**

3/4 **cup white chocolate chips (Nestlé)**

36 **thin pretzel sticks (Rold Gold, Bachman)**

6 **green fruit chews (Jolly Rancher, Laffy Taffy)**

6 **pink fruit chews (Starburst, Jolly Rancher, Laffy Taffy)**

1 **can (16 ounces) vanilla frosting**

Green and red food coloring

3/4 **cup green decorating sugar (Cake Mate)**

12 **yellow candy-coated chocolates (M&M's)**

1 **tube (4.25 ounces) chocolate decorating icing (Cake Mate)**

12 **light pink jelly beans (Jelly Belly)**

Granulated sugar to support cupcakes (optional)

Punch cups (optional)

1. If using the cookie dough, preheat the oven to 350°F and line two cookie sheets with parchment paper.

2. Roll out the dough following the directions on page 225 and cut 12 hat shapes using the template on page 192. Bake the cookies until just golden and firm to the touch, 7 to 10 minutes. Transfer to a wire rack and allow to cool completely. If using graham crackers, cut them in half crosswise with a small serrated knife.

Follow the template to cut a tall triangle from each (see photo, opposite page). Reserve the tall triangle and 1 trimmed piece to make the elf hats. Line two cookie sheets with wax paper. Arrange the larger graham pieces on the wax paper. Place the smaller graham pieces next to the larger grahams, near the top edge to make the hat shape (see photo, opposite page).

3. Place the white chocolate chips in a ziplock bag; do not seal the bag. Microwave for about 10 seconds to soften. Massage the mixture and return to the microwave. Repeat the process until the white chocolate is smooth, about 30 seconds (see page 18). Press out the excess air and seal. Snip a small ($1/8$-inch) corner from the bag and pipe a line along the short end of the smaller cookie piece. Attach to the side of the larger cookie to make the hat. Repeat with the remaining cookies.

4. Pipe some white chocolate in the center of the cookie hat and place 2 pretzel sticks side by side $3/4$ inch apart in the melted chocolate, allowing them to overhang the wide bottom edge by about 2 inches. Use an extra pretzel stick to support the overhanging pretzels while they harden (see photo, opposite page). Repeat with the remaining pretzel sticks. Refrigerate until set, about 5 minutes.

5. Roll out each green fruit chew on a clean work surface to a 1-by-1$1/2$-inch rectangle. For the hat brims, cut each rectangle in half lengthwise. Roll out the pink fruit chews to a $1/8$-inch thickness. For the ears, cut the pink chews into twenty-four 1-inch ovals. Pinch the short ends to form the ears.

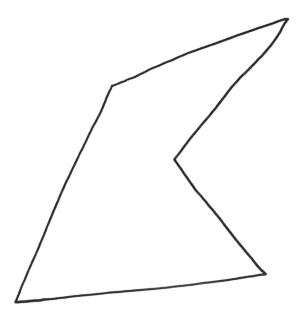

5. Tint ³/₄ cup of the vanilla frosting green with the food coloring. Place the green sugar in a small shallow bowl. Spread a thin layer of the green frosting on the flat side of a hat assembly. Dip the frosted side into the green sugar to coat. Repeat with the remaining hats. Spread a small line of green frosting on the bottom edge of the hats and add the green fruit chew brims, trimming the ends to fit. Attach the yellow candy at the tip of the hat with a dot of green frosting.

6. Tint 3 tablespoons of the vanilla frosting red with the red food coloring. Spoon the red frosting into a small ziplock bag. Spoon 3 tablespoons of the vanilla frosting into a small ziplock bag. Press out the excess air and seal the bags.

7. Tint the remaining vanilla frosting light pink with a drop or two of red food coloring. Spread the pink frosting on top of the cupcakes and smooth. Insert the pretzel ends of the hat assembly at one edge of the cupcake to secure. Snip a very small corner from each bag, with the red and white frosting. For open eyes, pipe 2 white dots; add a dot of chocolate decorating icing for the pupil. For closed or squinty eyes, pipe lines of decorating icing. Add a pink jelly bean, crosswise, for the nose. Pipe a squiggled red line as the mouth. Add the fruit chew for the ears. Spoon sugar into punch cups, if using, and add the cupcakes.

BLOW-UP LAWN SANTAS

Blow up Santa into a jumbo cupcake this year. With a jolly round belly filled with frosting, our overinflated Santa needs a Tootsie Roll belt and chocolate nonpareil buckle to ensure that his cupcake liner stays up.

8 jumbo vanilla cupcakes baked in red paper liners (see Sources)

8 mini vanilla cupcakes baked in red paper liners (see Sources)

16 white spice drops

$^1/_2$ cup granulated sugar

20 red spice drops

1 cup red decorating sugar (Cake Mate)

24 chocolate chews (Tootsie Rolls)

1 can (16 ounces) vanilla frosting

Red food coloring

16 mini chocolate chips

8 each pink and red candy decors (Cake Mate)

16 pink flat round sprinkles (Wilton)

16 green spice drops

8 chocolate nonpareil candies (Sno-Caps), plus more for the plates

16 chocolate creme-filled sandwich cookies (Oreos)

16 large malted milk balls

1. Press 2 white spice drops together and roll out on a clean work surface sprinkled with the granulated sugar to a $^1/_8$-inch thickness. Repeat with the remaining white spice drops. Cut out the beard shape with sharp scissors using the template (page 196). Reserve 4 red spice drops. Working with the remaining 16, press 2 of the spice drops together and roll out on a work surface coated with

some of the red decorating sugar, adding more red sugar when necessary, to a ⅛-inch thickness. Repeat with the remaining 14 red spice drops. Cut out 8 hat shapes with sharp scissors using the template below.

2. Soften 3 of the chocolate chews in the microwave for 3 seconds. Press the candies together and roll out into a rope about 9 inches long. For the belts, flatten the rope with a rolling pin to a ⅛-inch thickness and cut into a ½-by-9-inch strip. Repeat with the remaining 21 chocolate chews to make 8 belts.

3. Spoon ½ cup of the vanilla frosting into a ziplock bag, press out the excess air, and seal. Tint ½ cup of the vanilla frosting pale pink with the red food coloring and cover to prevent it from drying out. Tint the remaining vanilla frosting red with the red food coloring. Place the remaining red sugar in a small shallow bowl. Spread the red frosting on top of the jumbo cupcakes, mounding it slightly. Roll the tops of the cupcakes in the red sugar to cover completely (see page 17). Snip a small (⅛-inch) corner from the bag with the vanilla frosting. Pipe a few dots of vanilla frosting around the top edge of each jumbo cupcake. Attach the chocolate chew belt around the top edge, trimming any excess if necessary.

4. Spread the top of the mini cupcakes with the pink frosting and smooth. Add the white spice drop beard to one half of a mini cupcake and let it overhang slightly. Add the red spice drop hat on the opposite side of the mini cupcake, allowing it to overhang slightly. Add the mini chocolate chips for the eyes, pointed ends

beard

hat

down into the pink frosting. With the vanilla frosting, pipe a decorative edge along the straight edge of the hat using the beading technique (see page 13). Pipe a dot at the very tip of the hat. Pipe small dots of frosting and attach a pink candy decor for the nose, a red candy decor for the mouth, and 2 flat pink sprinkles for the cheeks. Repeat with the remaining mini cupcakes and candies.

5. Cut the 4 reserved red spice drops in half lengthwise with a small knife. Turn a decorated head on its side and place in the center of a jumbo cupcake. Place a red spice drop half behind the overhang of the hat for support. Pipe a dot of vanilla frosting on each side of the jumbo cupcake and add 2 green spice drops, flat side against the cupcake, as the mittens. Pipe a dot of vanilla frosting on the center of the chocolate chew belt and add the Sno-Cap candy as the buckle. Repeat with remaining cupcakes.

6. Arrange 2 chocolate sandwich cookies on a small plate, positioning them on top of each other and using a dot of vanilla frosting to secure together. For the boots, attach 2 malted milk balls in front of the cookies, using more frosting to secure. Place the Santa cupcake on top of the cookie assembly. Add additional Sno-Caps to the plate. Repeat with the remaining cupcakes.

BLUE POINSETTIAS

CUPCAKE

We'd sing "Blue Christmas" except that these poinsettias are too festive to be sad and too easy to save just for Christmas. We cut the petals from frosty blue Wintermint gum and placed them on cupcakes frosted in white. For a more traditional look, use Big Red gum and red paper liners.

12 **vanilla cupcakes baked in blue paper liners (see Sources)**

90 **sticks blue gum (Wrigley's Orbit Wintermint)**

1 **cup coarse white decorating sugar (see Sources)**

1¹/₂ **cups canned vanilla frosting**

36 **yellow mini candy-coated chocolates (M&M's Minis)**

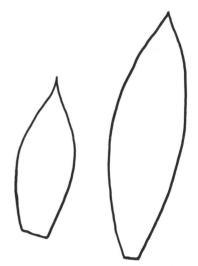

1. Working in small batches so the gum doesn't dry out before it is shaped, unwrap a few pieces at a time and cut with a clean pair of scissors following the petal templates at right. Gently pinch the flat end to make 60 large and 60 small petals. Allow the gum to dry for 30 minutes before assembling.

2. Place the white decorating sugar in a small shallow bowl. Spread the tops of the cupcakes with the vanilla frosting and smooth. Roll the edges of the cupcakes in the sugar (see page 17).

3. Arrange 10 to 12 petals of various sizes on top of each cupcake, inserting the pinched end of the gum slices in the center of the cupcake. Add 3 yellow candies in the center to make the poinsettias. Arrange the poinsettia cupcakes on a serving platter to make a wreath.

Makes 24 snowmen faces

FROSTY MUGS

We gave our snowmen a fresh face, rolling the frosting in sugar for extra sparkle. We added chocolate morsels for eyes, mini morsels for mouths, and orange fruit slices for carrot noses. The magic in the top hat comes from a chocolate wafer cookie.

24 **chocolate cupcakes baked in silver foil liners (Reynolds)**

1¼ **cups coarse white decorating sugar (see Sources)**

24 **thin chocolate cookies (Famous Chocolate Wafers)**

12 **orange candy fruit slices**

2 **cans (12 ounces each) fluffy vanilla frosting**

Green food coloring

¼ **cup chocolate chips**

¼ **cup mini chocolate chips**

Large red sprinkles

1. Place the white decorating sugar in a small shallow bowl. For the hats, using a serrated knife and angling it slightly inward from top to bottom, cut ¼ inch from opposite sides of the chocolate cookies. Reserve 24 of the smaller cookie pieces for the hat brims. For the noses, cut each orange fruit slice into two ¼-by-³/₄-by-³/₄-inch triangles.

2. Tint ¼ cup of the frosting green with the food coloring. Spoon the green frosting into a small ziplock bag, press out the excess air, and seal. Spread the remaining vanilla frosting on top of the cupcakes, mounding it slightly. Roll the tops in the decorating sugar to cover completely (see page 17).

3. Press the base of an orange candy nose into the center of each cupcake. Add the standard chocolate chips, pointed ends down, for the eyes. Add the mini chocolate chips, pointed ends down, as the mouth.

4. Right before serving, use a small paring knife to cut a slit in each cupcake, parallel to the edge. Insert the large cookie piece, small end in, as the hat. Add a smaller cookie piece, cut edge down, as the brim. Snip a small (¹/₈-inch) corner from the bag with the green frosting and pipe a decorative edge along the crown of the hat or pipe a few holly leaves and add a couple of red sprinkles.

OH TANNENBAUM

The long needles of our stunning pine centerpiece are green candy wafers drizzled from a ziplock bag. The star is crafted from melted hard candies.

24 **vanilla cupcakes baked in green paper liners (see Sources)**

1 **cup green candy melting wafers (Wilton)**

1 **can (16 ounces) vanilla frosting**

Green food coloring

2 **tablespoons white nonpareils, plus more for the platters (see Sources)**

¼ **cup red mini candy-coated chocolates (M&M's Minis) or small red cinnamon candies (Red Hots)**

1 **red candy star (page 204)**

1. Line three cookie sheets with wax paper. Place the green candy melting wafers in a ziplock bag; do not seal the bag. Microwave for about 10 seconds to soften. Massage the mixture and return to the microwave. Repeat the process until the candy is smooth, about 1 minute total (see page 18). Press out the excess air and seal the bag. Snip a small (⅛-inch) corner from the bag and pipe a continuous tight zigzag row, about 2½ inches wide and close together, down the length of a cookie sheet (see page 18). Make 2 more rows. Repeat to fill the remaining 2 cookie sheets. Refrigerate until set, about 5 minutes.

2. Tint the vanilla frosting green with the food coloring. Spread the tops of 4 cupcakes with green frosting, mounding it slightly in the center. Break the green candy zigzags into smaller pieces to look like pine needles. Place on top of the cupcakes, allowing the pine needles to overhang slightly. Add white nonpareils and a few red candies. Repeat with the remaining cupcakes, frosting, and candy.

3. Arrange cupcakes around the perimeter of a square platter. Arrange more cupcakes around the perimeter of a smaller square platter. Arrange 4 cupcakes close together on a small square plate. Set 1 cupcake on top, in the center of the 4 cupcakes. Add the red candy star in the center of the top cupcake, press-

ing into frosting to secure. Place small inverted glasses (tall enough to provide clearance for the cupcakes and needles) in the centers of the two larger platters, spaced to support the platter above. Place the middle-size platter on top of the glasses on the largest platter, and top off with the small plate with the star on top. Place any leftover cupcakes on small plates, positioning them around the tree. Add additional white nonpareils to the platters.

HOLIDAY'S BRIGHTEST STARS

Colorful candy stars make beautiful tree toppers. You can also make Hanukkah cupcakes by putting the stars on vanilla-frosted cupcakes baked in silver foil liners.

Hard candies: 4 red for the Christmas star; 40 blue for the Hanukkah stars (Jolly Rancher)

Metal star-shaped cookie cutters: one 2- to 3-inch five-pointed star cutter for the Christmas star; several six-pointed star cutters in a range of sizes from 1 to 3 inches for the Hanukkah stars

Vegetable cooking spray

1. Preheat the oven to 350°F. Line several cookie sheets with foil. Place the unwrapped hard candies in a ziplock bag; do not seal. Using a small hammer or the back of a saucepan, break the candies into small pieces. Sprinkle the candies in an even layer in the center of the prepared cookie sheets (see page 21).

2. Spray the cookie cutters with the vegetable cooking spray. Bake one cookie sheet at a time until the candies are just melted and smooth, 3 to 4 minutes. Transfer the cookie sheet to a wire rack. Immediately press the oiled cookie cutters, as close together as possible, into the melted candy. Let stand until the candy has cooled completely, about 5 minutes. Carefully break apart the candy sheet to remove the cutters and candy stars, reusing the candy scraps to break up for the next batch. Repeat with the other cookie sheets.

POLAR OPPOSITES

Polar bears and walruses refuse to float on the same ice floe, but we make them share a doughnut hole—for their bodies—then we let them drift their separate ways.

POLAR BEARS

12 vanilla cupcakes baked in white paper liners

1 can (16 ounces) vanilla frosting

1/2 cup canned chocolate frosting

12 plain doughnut holes

1 cup flaked sweetened coconut

60 white spice drops

24 frosted oat cereal O's (Frosted Cheerios)

12 brown mini candy-coated chocolates (M&M's Minis)

Blue and white rock candy for garnish (optional)

1. Spoon 1/2 cup of the vanilla frosting into a ziplock bag. Spoon the chocolate frosting into a ziplock bag. Press out the excess air and seal the bags. Spread the top of the cupcakes with some of the remaining vanilla frosting, mounding it slightly. Place a doughnut hole close to one edge of each frosted cupcake. Place the cupcakes in the freezer until firm, 15 to 20 minutes.

2. Pulse the coconut in a food processor until finely chopped or chop by hand with a knife. Place the coconut in a small shallow bowl.

3. Spread the remaining vanilla frosting in a thin layer over the doughnut hole and fill in the gap around the base to smooth (see photo, page 210). Roll the assembled cupcake in the chopped coconut to cover completely (see page 17). Repeat with the remaining cupcakes.

4. Snip a small (1/8-inch) corner from the bags with the vanilla and chocolate frostings. For the bottom paws, flatten 24 of the spice drops lengthwise. For each

cupcake, pipe dots of vanilla frosting on top of the coated doughnut hole and attach the cereal pieces as the ears. Pipe a line of vanilla frosting around the ears and coat with coconut. Pipe dots of vanilla frosting on the cupcake and attach 2 of the flattened spice drops as the bottom paws. Pipe dots of vanilla frosting and attach the flat side of spice drops as the muzzle on the doughnut hole and the front paws on the cupcake. Pipe the mouth, eyes, claws (using the squeeze-release-pull technique, page 13), and pads on the spice drops using the chocolate frosting. Add the brown candy as the nose.

WALRUSES

12 chocolate cupcakes baked in brown paper liners (see Sources)

1 can (16 ounces) chocolate frosting

12 plain doughnut holes

1 box (9 ounces) thin chocolate cookies (Famous Chocolate Wafers)

6 marshmallows

2 tablespoons white nonpareils (see Sources)

12 brown mini candy-coated chocolates (M&M's Minis)

Chocolate sprinkles

Blue and white rock candy for garnish (optional)

1. Spoon ½ cup of the chocolate frosting into a ziplock bag, press out the excess air, and seal. Spread the top of the cupcakes with some of the remaining chocolate frosting, mounding it slightly. Place a doughnut hole close to one edge of each frosted cupcake. Place the cupcakes in the freezer until firm, 15 to 20 minutes.

2. For the side flippers, using a serrated knife, cut 1 inch from each side of 12 of the chocolate cookies. For the tails, cut 6 of the chocolate cookies in half. Pulse the scraps and the remaining cookies in a food processor until fine, or place the cookies in a large ziplock bag and use a rolling pin to crush the cookies into fine crumbs. Place the cookie crumbs in a small shallow bowl. For the tusks, cut a ½-inch corner from each side of the short end of the marshmallows, making 4 tusks from each marshmallow. Repeat with the remaining marshmallows.

3. Spread the remaining chocolate frosting in a thin layer over the doughnut hole and fill in the gap around the base to smooth (see photo below). Roll the assembled cupcake in the cookie crumbs to cover completely. Repeat with the remaining cupcakes.

4. Snip a small (⅛-inch) corner from the bag with the chocolate frosting. For each cupcake, pipe 2 circles of frosting on the outer side of the coated doughnut hole for the snout. Insert the marshmallow tusks, rounded side out, into the frosting from below. Dip an index finger into the white nonpareils and lightly touch the nonpareils to the chocolate snout to adhere. Add a brown candy as the nose. Pipe dots of chocolate frosting on each side of the doughnut hole above the nose and add a chocolate sprinkle for each eye. Pipe dots of chocolate frosting and attach the small chocolate cookie pieces as the flippers on each side of the cupcake, rounded side down, and attach the cookie half as the tail at the back of the cupcake, straight edge down. Repeat with the remaining cupcakes. Arrange the cupcakes on a platter with the blue and white rock candy, if you desire.

ON COMET! ON CUPCAKE!

With Rudolph playing the hero, cupcake reindeer outfitted with chocolate antlers strain in their licorice harnesses and tracings, ready to dash away, dash away, dash away all.

9 vanilla cupcakes baked in white paper liners

9 mini vanilla cupcakes baked in white paper liners

$1/2$ cup dark cocoa candy melting wafers (Wilton)

2 tablespoons white nonpareils (see Sources)

1 can (16 ounces) vanilla frosting

1 teaspoon unsweetened cocoa powder (Hershey's)

$1^1/2$ cups brown decorating sugar (see Sources)

1 roll (0.75 ounce) strawberry fruit leather (Fruit by the Foot)

1 tube (4.25 ounces) chocolate decorating icing (Cake Mate)

8 brown mini candy-coated chocolates (M&M's Minis)

1 red mini candy-coated chocolate (M&M's Minis)

18 brown candy-coated chocolate-covered sunflower seeds (Sunny Seed Drops)

54 yellow flat round decorating sprinkles (Cake Mate)

White snowflake sprinkles (optional; see Sources)

6 strands red licorice laces (Twizzlers Pull-n-Peel)

1. Place the antler templates (page 213) on a cookie sheet and cover with wax paper. Place the dark cocoa candy melting wafers in a ziplock bag; do not seal the bag. Microwave for 10 seconds, massage the bag, and repeat the process until smooth, about 45 seconds total (see page 18). Press out the excess air and seal. Snip a very small ($1/16$-inch) corner from the bag and pipe the outline of the antlers. Sprinkle the melted candy with the white nonpareils while the candy is

still wet. Repeat to make 11 sets of antlers (the extra are in case of breakage). Refrigerate until set, about 5 minutes.

2. Tint the vanilla frosting light brown with the cocoa powder. Place the brown decorating sugar in a small shallow bowl. Spread the tops of all the cupcakes with the light brown frosting and smooth. Roll the tops of the frosted cupcakes in the sugar to cover completely (see page 17).

3. Cut the red fruit leather into 4-inch pieces. Cut each piece lengthwise into 1/2-inch-wide strips to make 9 pieces. Lay a strip of red fruit leather across the center of each of the standard cupcakes, adding a dot of chocolate decorating icing to secure (trim any excess overhang).

4. Pipe dots of chocolate decorating icing for the eyes and a dot for the nose on top of the mini cupcakes. Add the brown mini candies and the red mini candy as the noses. Turn each decorated head on its side and place on a body, pressing into the frosting to secure. Gently peel the chocolate antlers from the wax paper and arrange them on top of the mini cupcakes, pushing into the frosting to secure. Pipe a dot of chocolate decorating icing on the outside of each antler base and add candy-coated sunflower seeds as the ears.

5. For the harness bells, pipe 3 dots of chocolate decorating icing down the center of the fruit leather on each side of the cupcakes and attach the yellow sprinkles. Place the cupcakes on small plates and add the snowflake sprinkles, if desired. Arrange the cupcakes on their plates on a serving platter or the table with the red-nosed reindeer in the lead. Cut the red licorice laces and string them from harness to harness, securing with a dot of chocolate decorating icing.

GINGERBREAD VILLAGE

Anything you can do with a gingerbread house, we can do better with cupcakes. We turn our jumbo cupcakes (gingerbread, of course) on their sides and attach cookie bases and graham cracker roofs. You can make candy doors, cereal shingles, spice drop trees, and frosting icicles. Some of our favorite decorations are M&M's, red Twizzlers Pull-n-Peel licorice, white and yellow gum squares, chocolate-covered raisins, starlight mints, green Froot Loops, white jelly beans, snowflake sprinkles, red sour balls, thin pretzel sticks, red fruit leather, red sprinkles, Tootsie Rolls, Golden Grahams and Chex cereal, chocolate Sno-Caps, and flaked sweetened coconut — but use whatever you like. Welcome to your new holiday tradition.

5 **jumbo Gingerbread Cupcakes (page 222) baked in brown paper liners (see Sources)**

1 **can (16 ounces) plus 1 cup vanilla frosting**

   Red, green, and brown food coloring (see Sources)

1 **cup canned dark chocolate frosting**

2 **each red, green, yellow, and orange spice drops**

3 **tablespoons granulated sugar**

5 **whole graham crackers**

2 **vanilla creme wafers**

5 **marshmallows and/or candy spearmint leaves**

7 **dark chocolate nonpareil candies (Sno-Caps)**

   Assorted candies for decorating (see headnote)

1. Tint ¼ cup of the vanilla frosting red with the food coloring. Tint ½ cup of the vanilla frosting green with the food coloring. Spoon 1 cup of the vanilla frost-

ing into a ziplock bag. Spoon the red, green, and dark chocolate frostings into separate ziplock bags. Press out the excess air and seal the bags. Tint the remaining vanilla frosting light brown with the brown food coloring and spoon into a ziplock bag. Keep the frosting covered until ready to use.

2. For the doors, press 2 like-colored spice drops together and roll out on a work surface sprinkled with the granulated sugar to a $\frac{1}{8}$-inch thickness. Cut the flattened gumdrops into doors measuring about $\frac{3}{4}$ by $1\frac{1}{2}$ inches; cut off the top corners to create the rounded door.

3. For the house bases and roof pieces, using a serrated knife, cut 2 whole graham crackers, following the perforated lines, into 4 equal pieces each. Discard 1 piece; you will have 7 pieces. Cut the remaining 3 graham crackers into 6 pieces measuring 2 by $2\frac{1}{2}$ inches. For one of the roofs, cut $\frac{3}{4}$ inch on the diagonal from one short end of each of the 2 vanilla creme wafers.

4. Snip a small ($\frac{1}{8}$-inch) corner from each bag of frosting. Spread the top of the cupcakes with the light brown frosting. Add a flattened gumdrop door to 4 of the cupcakes.

5. Using frostings for the glue, pipe decorations and attach assorted candies to outline doors, make windows and rock walls, and create anything else you want on the façade of your house. Use pretzel sticks to make timbers (see photo, page 214).

6. Cut the marshmallow and/or spearmint leaves in half on the diagonal. Place a quartered piece of graham cracker on a small plate or platter. Pipe a dot of vanilla frosting in the center of the graham cracker. Place the front edge of a decorated cupcake on its side on top of the cracker. Use the cut marshmallows and/or spearmint leaves, cut side down, on either side of the cupcake as support. Pipe some of the light brown frosting along the top edge of each cupcake. For the roofs, add the 6 larger graham cracker pieces to 3 of the cupcakes, the chocolate nonpareil candies to 1 cupcake, and the vanilla creme wafers to the remaining cupcake, using the remaining quarter graham cracker pieces behind as supports.

7. Using frostings for the glue, add shingles, pipe icicles (using the squeeze-release-pull technique, page 13), and attach assorted candies or whatever else inspires you.

SNOW-COVERED TREES

6 mini vanilla cupcakes baked in white paper liners

5 vanilla cupcakes baked in white paper liners

1 can (16 ounces) vanilla frosting

6 white spice drops

2 tablespoons white nonpareils (see Sources)

2 tablespoons coarse white decorating sugar (see Sources)

1. Divide the vanilla frosting between two ziplock bags, press out the excess air, and seal. Snip a small (¹/₈-inch) corner from each bag. Remove the paper liners from 5 of the mini cupcakes. Pipe a dot of frosting on top of the standard cupcakes and add the unwrapped mini cupcakes, top side down, pressing into the frosting. Pipe a dot in the center of each upside-down mini cupcake and press a spice drop, flat side down, into the frosting. Pipe a dot of frosting in the center of the mini cupcake with the liner and press a spice drop flat side down into the frosting to make a mini tree. Pipe the vanilla frosting around the edge of each cupcake using the squeeze-release-pull technique (see page 13), and then work upward in concentric circles, always pulling the frosting away from the center and slightly overlapping the rows, until the cupcake and spice drop are completely covered. Repeat with the remaining cupcakes.

2. Sprinkle the tops of the frosted cupcakes with the white nonpareils and decorating sugar.

Cupcakes, Frostings, and Cookies

Like most folks, we're busy, and we definitely don't want to lose precious cupcaking time. That's why we rely on store-bought cake mix for our projects. We doctor the mix with buttermilk for flavor and add an egg to improve the structure. In addition to the perfect cake mix recipe, we have given you nine variations, adding extra ingredients to the different mixes. Feel free to use your favorite mixes, but avoid lighter ones like angel food or chiffon cake because they sink. If you have a favorite "scratch" recipe, go ahead and use it. To save time, we often make our cupcakes the day before, wrap them in plastic, and decorate them the next day. They stay nice and moist in the plastic wrap overnight.

We use store-bought frosting right out of the can for most projects. Store-bought frosting tints well, creating strong, vibrant colors, and it is the only frosting we trust for melting and dipping. But not all store-bought frostings are created equal. Make sure you avoid ones that are whipped, low-fat, or low-sugar; they don't hold up. Duncan Hines Creamy Home-Style frostings taste great, and the texture is consistently firm, making it easy to create the dips, sweeps, and peaks that look so appetizing.

When we have more time or just want to be able to say, "It's homemade," we turn to our own Almost-Homemade Buttercream, the base from which all our other flavors are built. We've given you eight flavors, all of them delicious, plus an almost-instant ganache for creating rich, shiny surfaces.

We have also included two recipes for working with store-bought refrigerated cookie dough. The simple addition of some flour or cocoa powder creates a dough that is easy to work with and bakes into nice firm cookies.

Cupcakes

Frostings

Cookies

PERFECT CAKE MIX CUPCAKES

Avoid cake mixes with pudding in the mix and lighter kinds such as angel food, since cupcaking requires firm cake. If you don't have buttermilk on hand, you can make a fair substitution by adding 1 tablespoon lemon juice to 1 cup whole milk. Let stand for 10 minutes to sour (real buttermilk is better).

1 box (18.25 ounces) cake mix (such as classic vanilla or devil's food)

1 cup buttermilk (in place of the water called for on the box)

Vegetable oil (the amount on the box)

4 large eggs (in place of the number called for on the box)

1. Preheat the oven to 350°F. Line muffin cups with paper liners.

2. Following the box's instructions, combine all the ingredients in a large bowl, using the buttermilk in place of the water specified (the box will call for more water than the buttermilk here), using the amount of vegetable oil that is called for (typically, white or yellow cake calls for ⅓ cup; chocolate cakes usually call for ½ cup), and adding the 4 eggs. Beat with an electric mixer until moistened, about 30 seconds. Increase the speed to high and beat until thick, 2 minutes longer.

3. Spoon half of the batter into a large ziplock bag, press out the excess air, and seal. Snip a ¼-inch corner from the bag and fill the paper liners two-thirds full (see page 10). Repeat with the remaining batter. Bake until golden (if using a light-colored cake mix) and a toothpick inserted in the center comes out clean, 20 to 25 minutes for jumbo, 15 to 20 minutes for standard, and 8 to 10 minutes for mini cupcakes. Remove the cupcakes from the baking pans, place on a wire rack, and allow to cool completely.

CHOCOLATE CHUNK SURPRISE

- **1 box (18.25 ounces) devil's food cake mix**
- **1 cup buttermilk**
- **$1/2$ cup vegetable oil**
- **4 large eggs**
- **12–24 caramel cream–filled chocolates (Milky Way Minis; halve if making mini cupcakes)**

Make as directed on page 220, submerging a caramel cream–filled chocolate into each muffin cup filled with batter.

CHOCOLATE-MINT

- **1 box (18.25 ounces) devil's food cake mix**
- **1 cup buttermilk**
- **$1/2$ cup vegetable oil**
- **4 large eggs**
- **$3/4$ cup chopped mint chocolates (Andes Crème de Menthe Thins)**

Make as directed on page 220, folding the chopped mint chocolates into the batter.

BANANA-CHOCOLATE

- **1 box (18.25 ounces) devil's food cake mix**
- **1 cup mashed bananas (about 3 medium)**
- **$3/4$ cup buttermilk**
- **$1/2$ cup vegetable oil**
- **4 large eggs**

Make as directed on page 220, adding the mashed bananas with the buttermilk and oil.

SPICE-RUM

- **1 box (18.25 ounces) spice cake mix**
- **2 tablespoons minced crystallized ginger**
- **1 teaspoon ground ginger**
- **$1/2$ teaspoon ground cinnamon**
- **$1/4$ teaspoon ground nutmeg**
- **Pinch ground cloves**
- **1 teaspoon rum extract**
- **1 cup buttermilk**
- **$1/3$ cup vegetable oil**
- **4 large eggs**

Make as directed on page 220, adding the minced ginger and spices to the cake mix and adding the rum extract with the buttermilk and oil.

cupcakes, frostings, and cookies ● 221

DOUBLE-TOP BANANA

1 box (18.25 ounces) banana supreme cake mix

1 cup mashed bananas (about 3 medium)

²/₃ cup buttermilk

¹/₃ cup vegetable oil

4 large eggs

Make as directed on page 220, adding the mashed bananas with the buttermilk and oil.

PUMPKIN-SPICE

1 box (18.25 ounces) classic vanilla cake mix

1 cup canned pumpkin (not pumpkin pie filling)

1 teaspoon pumpkin pie spice

³/₄ cup buttermilk

¹/₃ cup vegetable oil

4 large eggs

Make as directed on page 220, adding the canned pumpkin and pumpkin pie spice with the buttermilk and oil.

STRAWBERRY SUPREME

1 box (18.25 ounces) strawberry supreme cake mix

1 cup buttermilk

¹/₃ cup vegetable oil

4 large eggs

Make as directed on page 220.

ORANGE-SPICE

1 box (18.25 ounces) classic vanilla cake mix

1 cup buttermilk

¹/₃ cup vegetable oil

4 large eggs

2 teaspoons pumpkin pie spice

¹/₂ teaspoon grated orange peel

Make as directed on page 220, stirring the pumpkin pie spice and orange peel into the batter.

GINGERBREAD

1 box (18.25 ounces) classic vanilla cake mix

¹/₂ cup buttermilk

¹/₂ cup molasses

¹/₃ cup vegetable oil

4 large eggs

1¹/₂ teaspoons ground ginger

¹/₂ teaspoon ground cinnamon

¹/₄ teaspoon ground nutmeg

Make as directed on page 220, adding the molasses and spices

FROSTINGS

ALMOST-HOMEMADE VANILLA BUTTERCREAM

3 sticks (³/₄ pound) unsalted butter, cut into 1-inch pieces and softened

1 container (16 ounces) Marshmallow Fluff

¹/₂ cup confectioners' sugar, plus more if desired

1 teaspoon vanilla extract

1. Beat the butter in a large mixing bowl with an electric mixer on medium speed until light and fluffy. Add the Marshmallow Fluff and beat until smooth, scraping down the sides of the bowl. Add the confectioners' sugar and vanilla extract and beat until light and fluffy. If the mixture seems too stiff, soften in the microwave for no more than 10 seconds and beat well again until smooth.

2. Add up to 1 cup more confectioners' sugar to taste, if desired.

ORANGE BUTTERCREAM

1 teaspoon grated orange peel

Make as directed, beating in the orange peel until well blended.

GINGER-SPICE BUTTERCREAM

1 tablespoon finely minced crystallized ginger

1/2 teaspoon pumpkin pie spice

1/4 teaspoon ground ginger

Make as directed, beating in the crystallized ginger, pumpkin pie spice, and ground ginger until well blended.

ESPRESSO BUTTERCREAM

4 teaspoons instant espresso powder

1 tablespoon warm water

Make as directed, dissolving the espresso powder in the warm water and beating in until well blended.

RASPBERRY BUTTERCREAM

1/2 cup seedless raspberry jam

Make as directed, beating in the raspberry jam until well blended.

NUTELLA BUTTERCREAM

1/2 cup Nutella

Make as directed, beating in the Nutella until well blended.

PEANUT BUTTER BUTTERCREAM

1/2 cup creamy peanut butter

Make as directed, beating in the peanut butter until well blended.

HONEY BUTTERCREAM

1/4 cup honey

Make as directed, beating in the honey until well blended.

NEXT-TO-INSTANT GANACHE
Makes about 1 1/2 cups

1 can (16 ounces) chocolate or dark chocolate frosting

Spoon the frosting into a microwavable 2-cup measuring cup. Microwave on high, stopping to stir frequently, until the frosting has the texture of lightly whipped cream, 30 to 60 seconds.

QUICK SUGAR COOKIES

³/₄ cup all-purpose flour

1 tube (16.5 ounces) refrigerated sugar cookie dough

1. Preheat the oven to 350°F. Line two cookie sheets with parchment paper.

2. Knead the flour into the dough on a clean work surface until smooth. Divide the dough in half. Roll out each piece on a lightly floured surface to a ¹/₄-inch thickness. Cut out the desired shapes according to the recipe, cutting as close together as possible, using templates or a homemade cookie cutter. Transfer the shapes to the prepared pans, spacing about 1 inch apart. Remove the center areas of the cookies if directed in the recipe.

3. Bake until golden and firm to the touch, 7 to 12 minutes depending on the size and shape of the cookies. Transfer to a wire rack and cool completely.

CHOCOLATE SUGAR COOKIES

¹/₃ cup all-purpose flour

¹/₄ cup unsweetened cocoa powder

1 tube (16.5 ounces) refrigerated sugar cookie dough

1. Preheat the oven to 350°F. Line two cookie sheets with parchment paper.

2. Knead the flour and cocoa powder into the dough on a clean work surface until smooth. Divide the dough in half. Roll out each piece on a lightly floured surface to a ¹/₄-inch thickness. Cut out the desired shapes according to the recipe, cutting as close together as possible, using templates or a homemade cookie cutter. Transfer the shapes to the prepared pans, spacing about 1 inch apart. Remove the center areas of the cookies if directed in the recipe.

3. Bake until golden and firm to the touch, 7 to 12 minutes depending on the size and shape of the cookies. Transfer to a wire rack and cool completely.

SOURCES

BAKING SUPPLIES

Ateco
> (800) 645-7170
> www.atecousa.net

Offset spatulas. *A good source for cake decorating tools.*

Beryl's
P.O. Box 1584
North Springfield, VA 22151
> (703) 256-6951
> (800) 488-2749
> www.beryls.com

A wide variety of cupcake paper liners, as well as many other cupcake decorating supplies.

Cake Mate
> www.cakemate.com

A complete list of sugar and sprinkles available at your local grocery store, as well as creative cupcake ideas.

Candyland Crafts
201 West Main Street
Somerville, NJ 08876
> (908) 685-0410
> (877) 487-4289
> www.candylandcrafts.com

A great selection of cupcake decorating supplies.

Confectionery House
> (518) 279-4250
> (518) 279-3179
> www.confectioneryhouse.com

Solid-color cupcake paper liners. *A wide variety of melting chocolate wafers, sprinkles, food coloring, and luster dust.*

Country Kitchen SweetArt
4621 Speedway Drive
Fort Wayne, IN 46825
> (260) 482-4835
> (800) 497-3927
> www.countrykitchensa.com

Sanding and coarse sugars. *A wide variety of candy decors, sprinkles, luster dust, chocolate melting wafers, food coloring, and paper liners.*

Duncan Hines
> www.duncanhines.com

A complete list of cake mixes and frostings available at your local grocery store, as well as creative cupcake ideas and tips and ideas for baking.

Fancy Flours
> www.fancyflours.com

Beautiful and elegant cupcake supplies, from paper liners to specialty sugars, sprinkles, and decorations.

India Tree Gourmet Spices & Specialties
1421 Elliott Avenue West
Seattle, WA 98119
> (206) 270-0293
> (800) 369-4848
> www.indiatree.com

Beautiful coarse and decorating sugars. India Tree products are also available in some grocery stores.

Kitchen Krafts
P.O. Box 442
Waukon, IA 52172
> (563) 535-8000
> (800) 298-5389
> www.kitchenkrafts.com

A wide variety of decorating supplies.

McCormick
> www.mccormick.com

A great source for large-size food coloring and hard-to-find colors like neon and black and a strong selection of seasonal cupcake ideas. The color wheel on the food-color section of the site makes it easy to create custom colors.

New York Cake & Baking Supplies
56 West 22nd Street
New York, NY 10010
> (212) 675-2253
N.Y. Cake West
10665 W. Pico Blvd.
Los Angeles, CA 90064
> (310) 481-0875
> (877) NY-CAKE-8
> www.nycake.com

Food coloring, chocolate melting wafers, luster dust, dragées, sugars, sprinkles, and some paper liners.

Sugarcraft
2715 Dixie Highway
Hamilton, OH 45015
> (513) 896-7089
> www.sugarcraft.com

A wide variety of baking and decorating supplies.

Sur La Table
(800) 243-0852
www.surlatable.com
Crinkle cutters. *Bakeware, tiered cake stands, and schedules of decorating classes at stores.*

Wilton Industries
2240 West 75th Street
Woodbridge, IL 60517
(630) 963-1818
(800) 794-5866
www.wilton.com
A wide variety of baking supplies, including chocolate melting wafers, food coloring, paper liners, assorted sprinkles and sugars, and much more. Wilton products are also available in many craft and party stores and some grocery stores.

PARTY AND CRAFT SUPPLIES

A.C. Moore
www.acmoore.com
Marvy paper punch, plastic eggs. *Cake-decorating supplies and crafts, as well as books. Store locations are listed online.*

Beadalon
www.beadalon.com
Offset tweezers. *A great source for sorting trays and crafting mats.*

Fiskars
www.fiskars.com
Craft scissors. *Creative craft ideas, seminars, and products.*

Fred & Friends
www.worldwidefred.com
Finger Food plates. *Also other novelty items. Store locations are listed online.*

Michael's Craft Stores
(800) 642-4235
www.michaels.com
Marvy paper punch, plastic eggs. *A wide variety of craft supplies and cake-decorating supplies, including Wilton products.*

Paper Source
www.paper-source.com
Beautiful papers and crafting supplies, packing material, and boxes for cupcake gifts.

Reynolds
www.reynoldskitchens.com
The latest seasonal paper and foil liner selections, as well as a selection of creative cupcake ideas.

Tower Hobbies, K&S Brass Supplies
(217) 398-3636
(800) 637-6050
www.towerhobbies.com
Thin brass strips for making cookie cutters. *Other craft supplies.*

Ziploc
www.ziploc.com
Product information, as well as coupons for Ziploc products.

GOURMET CANDY SUPPLIES

Balboa Candy
301-A Marine Avenue
Balboa Island, CA 92662
(949) 723-6099
www.balboacandy.com
A great candy selection, specializing in retro candies and taffy.

Dylan's Candy Bar
1011 Third Avenue
New York, NY 10021
(866) 9-DYLANS
www.dylanscandybar.com
A wide variety of candies, including seasonal offerings.

Economy Candy
108 Rivington Street
New York, NY 10002
(800) 352-4544
www.economycandy.com
A good source for old-fashioned and bulk candies.

Jelly Belly Candy Company
One Jelly Belly Lane
Fairfield, CA 94533
(800) JB-BEANS
www.jellybelly.com
The largest selection available of gourmet jelly beans, including bulk sizes of individual flavors. The website includes a selection of creative cupcake ideas.

Old Time Candy Company
(866) WAX-LIPS
www.oldtimecandy.com
An interesting selection of nostalgic and novelty candies; large or small quantities can be purchased.

Sunflower Food & Spice Company
13318 West 99th Street
Lenexa, KS 66215
(913) 599-6448
(800) 377-4693
www.sunflowerfood
company.com
Sunny Seed Drops. *A wide variety of colors of candy-coated chocolate-covered sunflower seeds.*

Sweet Factory
2000 East Winston Road
Anaheim, CA 92806
(877) 817-9338
www.sweetfactory.com
A great selection of hard-to-find candies. Online and retail locations nationwide.

Karen Tack is the coauthor of the *New York Times* best-selling *Hello, Cupcake!* She is a cooking teacher and a food stylist and has created cupcakes and other desserts for the covers of many of America's top magazines, including *Bon Appétit, Gourmet, Cook's Illustrated, Good Housekeeping, Family Circle, Every Day with Rachael Ray, Woman's Day, Martha Stewart Living, Parents, Real Simple, FamilyFun,* and *All You.*

Alan Richardson is the coauthor of the *New York Times* best-selling *Hello, Cupcake!* He is also the coauthor of *The Breath of a Wok,* which won two prestigious awards from the International Association of Culinary Professionals (IACP). His photographs appear in dozens of best-selling cookbooks and leading food magazines.

OUR WEBSITE

www.hellocupcakebook.com
www.whatsnewcupcake.com

Visit our website to see our latest cupcake designs, to get information on the newest candies, as well as updates on demonstrations, events, and book signings, and to fill us in on your own cupcaking adventures.

Follow us on Twitter (@whatsnewcupcake)
to hear what we are saying about cupcakes right now.